Families at School
A Handbook for Parents

Adele Thomas
Brock University
St. Catharines, Ontario, Canada

Lynn Fazio
District School Board of Niagara
St. Catharines, Ontario, Canada

Betty L. Stiefelmeyer
District School Board of Niagara
St. Catharines, Ontario, Canada

International Reading Association
800 Barksdale Road, PO Box 8139
Newark, Delaware 19714-8139, USA
www.reading.org

Director of Publications   Joan M. Irwin
Assistant Director of Publications   Jeanette K. Moss
Senior Editor   Matthew W. Baker
Assistant Editor   Janet S. Parrack
Assistant Editor   Tori Mello
Publications Coordinator   Beth Doughty
Association Editor   David K. Roberts
Production Department Manager   Iona Sauscermen
Art Director   Boni Nash
Electronic Publishing Supervisor   Wendy A. Mazur
Electronic Publishing Specialist   Anette Schütz-Ruff
Electronic Publishing Specialist   Cheryl J. Strum
Electronic Publishing Assistant   Peggy Mason

Project Editor   Anne Fullerton

Photo Credits   Cleo Freelance Photography, cover

Library of Congress Cataloging in Publication Data
Thomas, Adele, 1942–
    Families at school: A handbook for parents/Adele Thomas,
Lynn Fazio, Betty L. Stiefelmeyer.
        p.   cm.
    Includes bibliographical references.
    1. Family literacy programs—Canada.   2. Home and school—Canada.
3. Reading—Parent participation.   I. Fazio, Lynn.   II. Stiefelmeyer, Betty L.
III. Title.
LC151.T563   1999   99-26395
371.19—dc21
ISBN 0-87207-248-7

Contents

Acknowledgments

Our program, a school-based family literacy initiative that invites parents to collaborate in learning with their children, represented a change in thinking for educators in our district and a significant commitment of staff and physical resources from the community. There are many demands made on educational institutions, but we have been fortunate to find numerous partners willing to make concerted efforts to realize family literacy goals.

Our original exploration of options for development of the program was supported by the Social Sciences and Humanities Research Council of Canada and by the National Literacy Secretariat of Human Resources and Development Canada. Throughout the development period, the District School Board of Niagara (Ontario, Canada) offered another source of support. We wish to acknowledge individuals within the district administration: Sandra White and Tillie Clapp, school board superintendents, whose creative energy and dedication to family literacy were instrumental in opening school doors for our program; and Judy Reid, coordinator of adult programs at Niagara Falls Secondary School, who provided ongoing assistance as we became part of school life. From their efforts we learned that the commitment of individuals really can have an impact on educational change.

Sincere appreciation is expressed to the Branscombe Family Foundation of Niagara Falls for its unstinting support in providing funding essential to the preschool program. Time and again, when public funding for child care did not materialize, the Branscombe Family Foundation filled our need. Without its commitment to families and community, our program would not have survived.

Community support for the program has been essential, and we gratefully acknowledge the generosity of organizations that donated resources and facilities. Cooperative agreements with the school board, community and social services, the local library system, and regional health services have made it possible to house several programs at the school. Thanks to such agreements, the family literacy program has benefited from a stable and comfortable site, and we have been able to concentrate fund-raising efforts on obtaining support for other aspects of the program's operation. Notably, financial support from the Niagara Falls Kiwanis Club allowed us to hire additional child-care staff and obtain program materials.

Our most profound gratitude is extended, however, to the families who have participated in the program, from whom we have learned so much. All have generously shared a portion of their lives with us, and they have genuinely cared about the overall goals of the program. Not only have the parents been our partners in developing the program's content and instructional strategies, but they also have collaborated in recruitment and public relations work, spreading the word about the program whenever they could. Their outreach has done more for family literacy in our community than we ever could have accomplished on our own.

Finally, special thanks go to our editor, Anne Fullerton. Her suggestions for streamlining and clarifying sections of the book were invaluable to us.

Introduction

Over the last several years we have been involved with parents and their children in a literacy program that focuses on the family. In the Niagara Falls Secondary School Family Learning Program, parents learn about reading and writing with their children, and at the same time improve their own literacy and parenting skills while earning high school credit. The children take part in a preschool program, with time for free play with other children and for activities with their parents.

When we first began thinking about a program for parents and caregivers, family literacy was a new idea for schools. We knew that parents were very motivated and committed to participating in their children's literacy development and hoped that their children would do well in school. We also knew that there were parents in our community who had dropped out of school themselves or had given up some of their own ambitions for education and career because of their personal situations and the demands of caring for their children. Our idea was to offer a program in which school would be a welcoming place, where parents could bring their children, advance their own educations, meet and get to know other parents, and learn ways to support their children's learning, all at the same time. The idea proved to be very popular with families.

Our program takes place every afternoon at a high school in a mid-sized Canadian city. Each semester, we have about 15 parents and their children. The children are toddlers and preschoolers, and the parents are most often single mothers from about 17 to 30 years old. We start each program session with "circle time," a chance for some group songs and games. Then the children move to their own activities in our play room. There they can do such things as color or paint, play with small toys and games, ride tricycles, and climb and slide on our indoor play equipment, all under the supervision of a trained early childhood education teacher.

For the next 2 hours, while their children are busy learning by playing, the parents are involved in learning of their own. In our program, we celebrate the fact that parents are their children's first and most important teachers. To help our parents learn more about their teaching role, we focus on how they can support children's literacy development and work out ways to improve their parenting skills. Parents read and discuss children's literature, find out about ways to read with their children, create their own children's games and activities, discuss ways of solving parenting problems, and learn about family nutrition. They write in journals, create their own children's books, and do parenting projects. They have many opportunities to talk with other parents in the group, and they collaborate with us in designing program activities and evaluation. All of these activities lead to their earning two high school credits.

At the end of the day, the parents and children are together again in the play room. They get a chance to share what they have been doing, and the parents try some of the things they have learned during their time on their own. Usually family literacy learning continues into the evening, once the parents and children return home.

This book grew out of experiences in our program. There are, of course, many different ways of being involved in family literacy. We have therefore tried to adapt our ideas and activities so they will be useful for any parent or caregiver who is interested in developing his or her own literacy while extending the literacy development of children at home. Whether you are taking part in a program like ours, going to a drop-in center or workshop, or simply looking for family literacy activities to do on your own at home, we hope you will find useful information here.

In Chapter 1, we discuss what is meant by the term *family literacy*. Besides giving some definitions, we describe the ways you are already helping your child learn about language, maybe without even knowing it. We also give details about different types of programs and suggest things to think about if you are trying to decide which approach might be best for you.

Chapter 2 introduces ideas about parents and children doing things together—the heart of family literacy. Playing with children is the focus here, and we give some suggestions about songs and games to try. We also talk about ways to play with children that can help make sure this special time is successful.

Chapter 3 presents more than 30 ready-to-use activities. Each one includes complete instructions and ideas for thinking about the learning it helps promote. All of these activities were developed and used by parents in the Family Learning Program. Parents who want to create new activities will find suggestions about things to keep in mind, along with a list of resources that might help.

In Chapter 4, the focus is on reading with young children. Different types of children's books are introduced, and we give an extensive list of titles that have been popular with the families in our program. Activities are included to guide parents through different reading strategies they can use when they read with children. We also describe books you can make and share together.

Chapter 5 takes a closer look at parenting. We stress how parents can use their own literacy skills to assist in resolving parenting concerns. Ideas for journal writing, sharing concerns with other parents, and steps to problem solving are provided, along with a list of recommended resources.

Parents of young children face new challenges every day as they work to meet the social, emotional, and physical needs of their growing children. Family literacy activities and resources offer one way to make the job a little easier.

Chapter 1

What Is Family Literacy?

Every day as you, your children, and other members of your family go about eating, getting ready for school or work, running errands, doing chores, playing, and relaxing together, you use language in different ways. Of course, you talk and listen to each other. But maybe you also read labels while shopping, recognize road signs while traveling around town, draw pictures and write stories together, read the cereal box, figure out the instructions for a new game, or share books and magazines. You rely on communication and the print around you to help your children understand things that are going on in your world.

At the same time, there is reading and writing that you do on your own. You might read the newspaper and talk with another adult about something in it, make a shopping list, use a recipe, write a letter, check instructions for household equipment, or take time to relax with a good book. But these things affect your children, too, because when they see you using your own literacy, they learn about the value of reading and writing.

These images are at the heart of what we call "family literacy." There is no single definition of the term, but generally it describes the many ways that families develop and use literacy in day-to-day tasks and activities. It can involve the reading, writing, speaking, and listening that parents do on their own or with other adults, children's independent explorations in language learning, and parents and children using literacy together. Usually it includes all these things.

Researchers who work in education have become very interested in the way family literacy affects how children learn to use language. Neither family, school, nor individual ability alone can fully account for a young child's literacy achievement. However, we do know that family interaction has a great impact on how easily children learn to read and write later, when they begin school. The family's role in this begins at the child's birth. Simply by hearing parents and caregivers talk, the child learns how words describe the everyday things in the world. Later she learns to talk herself, and begins to figure out how to use language to convey needs and to share interests with a parent. Later still—maybe after hundreds or even thousands of times spent listening to stories, drawing and labeling pictures, and noting signs when shopping or traveling—the child realizes that words can be written down. She starts to recognize letters and maybe even reads her own name or the word on the stop sign at the end of the street. Later still, young children who share reading with their parents learn about how books tell stories and give information. Their understanding of their own world grows, and they begin to imagine places and things beyond their immediate experiences.

Parents as Teachers

It is clear that literacy begins in the family, and that parents and other caregivers are each child's first and most important teachers. But how do families carry out this teaching job? Is it enough just to be positive about your child's reading and writing, or are there specific things you can do to help your child's literacy development?

A happy atmosphere, where parent and child spend time together playing and talking, is the foundation for literacy development. But other things are important, too:

- *The literacy environment*

  Does your child see you reading and writing? Are there books, magazines, pens, crayons, and other literacy materials in your home?

- *Parental teaching*

  How often do you teach your child something directly, maybe while you're reading together or doing homework? Do you point out new things? Are you patient when you answer questions?

- *Parental education*

  How much education do you have? Was school a positive or negative experience for you?

- *Opportunities to learn*

  What do you do to promote your child's learning? Does she get to meet lots of different people? Do you do different activities with her? Do you try not to leave her to do things on her own (such as watch television without your company) for long periods? Do you have a lot of different interests yourself?

- *Parental expectations*

  Do you expect your child to do well at school? Does your child know what you expect?

In terms of actually teaching children to read and write, it is clear that parents who read themselves and who read frequently with their young children are doing a great deal. Their children learn about print in a way that is fun and relaxed. This natural learning means that these children come to school already understanding key things about literacy. They know

- that reading and writing are fun,
- that print is useful,
- that stories and books work in certain ways,
- how to ask questions and think about what is in books, and
- about letters and how to recognize and understand words.

Family Literacy Programs

Obviously, almost all parents hope their children will do well in school, and most want to do everything they can to help them. Schools usually suggest that parents help their children by reading with them at home. But for parents who don't know much about children's books or how children learn to read, aren't confident about their own reading, or are nervous about things related to school, this suggestion is not very practical. These parents might find a family literacy program helpful. Perhaps the words of one young mother best sum up why parents get involved in these programs:

> I always had trouble with reading, and didn't like school. I left as soon as I could. I regret it now, but I want to make sure my child doesn't go through what I did. I'll try anything that will help her.

Types of Programs

Because of what we have learned about the vital role families play in children's literacy development, schools and community organizations are now actively looking for ways to promote family literacy. Whether your community is small and rural or urban and multicultural, there is probably some sort of family literacy initiative going on somewhere.

Ruth Nickse, a well-known researcher on literacy issues, classifies family literacy programs according to four types of learner participation:

1. Parents and children are both taught literacy skills.
2. Parents are taught literacy skills directly, in ways that will help them help their children at home.
3. Parents are asked by schools to participate in their children's literacy learning in specific ways.
4. Parents and children participate in literacy activities in the community (story time at the local library or "celebrate literacy" activities in a shopping mall, for example), but there is little or no direct instruction.

Our focus in this book is on both parents and children, and our own Family Learning Program uses the first two of these approaches.

Programs that adopt the first approach often use a format developed by the U.S. National Center for Family Literacy. This type of program brings parents and children together to learn and play. The emphasis is on literacy activities that can be done at home or in school. The group meets as a whole for some portion of the program day, but at other times the adults attend classes themselves while the children are involved in a preschool program. Besides working toward a particular educational goal (high school credit, for example), the parents receive support, information, and referrals, and they develop problem-solving skills for dealing with critical issues in their lives. Participation in such programs has been shown to have the following benefits:

- increases in the developmental skills of preschool children and in their readiness to begin school;
- gains in the educational level of parents;
- improvements in self-confidence of parents, particularly in terms of how they deal with their children's schooling; and
- improvements in parenting skills and in the way parents and children relate to each other.

In the second type of program, the emphasis is on skills for adults that will help them with their children's literacy. These programs might teach parents about children's books, combined with discussion of reading tips and answers to parents' questions about reading with their children. The idea is that by practicing with children's books, parents learn literacy skills that are directly related to their hopes for their own children's learning.

Getting Started in Family Literacy

Literacy in your family is obviously very personal, and how you decide to pursue it will depend mostly on your personal and family situation. You may decide to do some things on your own at home, and we hope that this book will give you some suggestions. Or you might start going to the story time at the local bookstore or visiting the library with your child as part of your regular weekly routine.

If you do think a more formal family literacy program is for you, the first thing to do is to figure out what you want to gain from it. Do you want to learn how to help your child be ready for or do better in school? Do you want to improve your own literacy skills? Do you need time away from your child? Would you rather learn and play with your child together? Do you want to meet other parents? Does your child need to learn about being with other children?

Once you have decided your goals, try to find out what programs might be available in your community. The local public library, social services agencies, local churches, community organizations (such as the YMCA), and elementary or high schools are good places to start gathering information. Most of these will be able to give you details of what they have to offer over the telephone. If they don't offer programs themselves, they will probably be able to tell you who in your area does.

When you know what's in your community, see if you can arrange to visit any of the programs that sound right for you. On a visit, you and your child should be able to meet with the teachers, see the layout of the site and the family learning area, and find out more about the program. But whether you are visiting or simply talking with a member of the program staff on the telephone, make sure you get answers to your questions, big and small. Will the program be flexible enough to meet your needs? Is there a lot of opportunity for active participation? How many people are in the group? Can you get help one on one if you need it? What is the schedule? What are the expectations for out-of-class assignments? How will you get there? What sort of training do the staff members have? What about disciplining the children if someone misbehaves? What facilities are there for snacks or diaper changing? Any question you have is a legitimate one.

Whether you are already involved in a program, looking for one, or starting out on some family literacy activities on your own, we hope this chapter has given you an idea of the great thing you are doing by becoming more involved with your child's literacy. In the chapters that follow you will find information and activities to help you as you begin on the road of reading, writing, learning, and sharing with your child.

Chapter 2

Parents and Children Together

My dishes went unwashed today. I didn't make my bed.
I took his hand and followed, where his eager footsteps led.
Oh yes, we went adventuring, my little child and I,
Exploring all the great outdoors beneath the sun and sky.
We watched a robin feed her young. We climbed a sunlit hill,
Saw cloud-sheep scamper through the sky. We plucked a daffodil.

Author Unknown

At the heart of family literacy is time devoted to parents and children doing things together. Children learn about literacy from adults who talk and play with them, sharing what they know about the world. At these times, the child is encouraged to discover, name, and explain, but the parent learns, too, because he or she is challenged to use language and problem-solving skills that fit with the child's stage of development.

This chapter gives ideas to help parents make literacy learning part of the everyday routine with their young children. The play activities we suggest help encourage children's language development, but they also give parents the chance to see how their children are growing in social, emotional, and intellectual areas. These activities are suggestions only, of course, and each parent will be able to come up with ideas to adapt them to his or her own family.

Opportunities to Be Together

In our Family Learning Program, parents and children are together for circle time and play room time every day. Circle time is a great way for all the parents and children to get to know one another while talking, singing, and playing in a relaxed atmosphere. Over time, as children watch and imitate, parents notice how their children are developing language, beginning to understand concepts, learning to make choices and take turns, and making friends. And when parents see how fast children learn the songs, how attentive and cooperative they are when singing and playing games, they quickly realize just how much their children can do. At the end of the day in play room time (and often continuing later at home), parents and children do fun activities that the parents have designed earlier in class. Here again, the parents have a chance to see how their children are growing and developing, and they also get ideas about talking and playing with their children by watching the others in the group.

Circle Time

Circle time is a common part of many day-care, preschool, and play-group programs. It is a time when parents sit with their children in a circle to sing songs or play word or finger games, or to do short group activities. In our program, parents and their children can read together quietly while other group members are arriving and getting settled. Then, circle time starts with a song to welcome everyone. Next, the children talk about the weather. We have cards with pictures of different types of weather, and children pick and describe the cards they think best fit the day. Sometimes the parents give hints by mentioning things that they noticed while they were walking or driving to school or that they see when they look out the window. We then sing a song about the days of the week and the weather, and we use day and number cards to fill in the date on a large calendar. One of the children usually helps with these jobs.

Our program is organized around themes and topics, and many of the things we do each day are related to them. In circle time at the beginning of each week, we introduce new songs and games related to that week's theme. Parents do the songs or games with their own children, and this gives them a chance to work together. The parents help their children figure out things and learn new skills, and have lots of chances to tell them what a good job they're doing.

Here are some of the games and songs we have used that have been popular with both the adults and the children. Each is related to one of our themes. Many of our circle time songs were adapted from Jean Warren's *Piggyback Songs for School*. Sources of songs and movement games appear in the "Circle Time Resources" list.

Numbers. We play "The Spotted Dinosaur." Each parent-child pair receives a picture of a dinosaur and a marker. We pass around a bag full of pennies, and each child takes a few. The parent and child then count the pennies and draw that number of spots on the dinosaur. Afterward, we all sing "Five Little Monkeys" together:

> Five little monkeys jumping on the bed,
> One fell off and bumped his head.
> Mama called the doctor, and the doctor said,
> "No more monkeys jumping on the bed."
> Four little monkeys jumping on the bed,
> One fell off and bumped his head....

Shapes. We make large shapes (such as squares or triangles) on the floor with masking tape. Then we all sing a version of "Old MacDonald Had a Farm," but instead of animals, "on his farm, he had some shapes." When we sing, "With a triangle here and a triangle there," for example, parents and children find a triangle to stand on together or find something triangle shaped in the room. Later, the children find a favorite shape to lie on (and then to hop in) as "See the Sleeping Bunnies" is sung:

> See the little bunnies,
> sleeping 'til it's noon.
> Shall we go and wake them
> with a merry tune?
> Sleep so still.
> Are they ill?
> Wake up little bunnies,
> hop, hop, hop.

Circle Time Resources

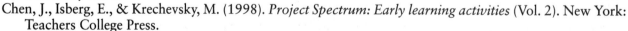

Beck, I., & Williams, S. (1994). *Round and round the garden.* Oxford, UK: Oxford University Press.

Chen, J., Isberg, E., & Krechevsky, M. (1998). *Project Spectrum: Early learning activities* (Vol. 2). New York: Teachers College Press.

Logson, B., Alleman, L., Straits, S., Belka, D., & Clark, D. (1997). *Physical education unit plans for preschool–kindergarten.* Champaign, IL: Human Kinetics.

Totline Staff. (1994). *1001 rhymes and fingerplays.* Everett, WA: Totline.

Traugh, S. (1993). *Music and movement in the classroom* (preK–K). Cypress, CA: Creative Teaching Press.

Warren, J. (1992). *Piggyback songs for school.* Everett, WA: Totline.

Wilmes, L., & Wilmes, D. (1992). *More everyday circle times.* Elgin, IL: Building Blocks.

Wake up little bunnies,
hop, hop, hop.
Wake up little bunnies,
hop and stop.

Colors. Each parent-child pair is given a "bingo" card with nine squares drawn on it and a few markers (such as coins or acorns). Each square is one of six colors that match the colors on the sides of a large die the whole class shares. Each child takes a turn rolling the die and naming the color that lands face up. When the color is named, pairs put a marker on that color on their cards. When a pair fills a whole card, the child shouts, "Bingo!" (This also can be played with shapes.) We then sing a color song that also reminds us about the weather and the names of the children in our group: "Who is wearing green pants, green pants, green pants on this rainy day? Mary is wearing green pants, green pants, green pants on this rainy day...."

Me, myself, and I. As the teacher calls out a body part, everyone touches that part. This can be a lot of fun if directions are added so that the parent and child work together—for example, "Touch each other's hands through your legs." We then sing the popular action song "If You're Happy and You Know It" or "The Hokey Pokey." Another possibility is "Where Is Thumbkin?":

Where Is Thumbkin?
Where is Thumbkin?
Here I am. [Singers stick one thumb out from a closed fist.]
Here I am. [Other thumb is stuck out.]
How are you today, sir? [One thumb "bows" to the other.]
Very well, I thank you. [The other thumb "bows."]
Run away. [One thumb "hides" again in a fist.]
Run away. [The other thumb "hides."]
Where is pointer?...

School fun. Parent-child pairs are given a sheet of paper with a line down the middle and a pen or pencil. At the top of one column is the word *Same* and the other is labeled *Different*. Parents and children walk around the room making a list of things they see that are the same as they have at home (for example, table, chair, stapler, crayons) and things that are different (such as bulletin boards or binders). We usually suggest that parents look particularly for things that are the same, because finding them makes the children feel more comfortable. We then sing and act out "The Wheels on the Bus," because many of our families come to school by bus:

The wheels on the bus go 'round and 'round,
'round and 'round, 'round and 'round.
The wheels on the bus go 'round and 'round,

All through the town.
The horn on the bus goes beep, beep, beep....

Senses. Parents and children use all five senses to explore the room. Parents ask questions such as, "Can you find something that smells nice?" We then sing a version of "Here We Go 'round the Mulberry Bush," in which everyone does an action when we sing, "This is the way I smell with my nose, smell with my nose, smell with my nose" or "This is the way I look with my eyes...."

Transportation. We give each parent and child a sheet of paper with pictures of a car, van, transport truck, bike, and airplane down one side. They then look out the window or go outside (depending on the weather) and make a stamp or some sort of mark to show the number of each thing that they see. Parents then can help children make a graph. To emphasize safety outside, we say this rhyme:

> Stop, look, and listen,
> Before you cross the street.
> Use your eyes, use your ears,
> And then use your feet.

Green and growing. We make large flower petals out of paper and draw designs on them. Each parent-child pair looks for other pairs who have the same design and try to make a flower. We then sing a song about nature, such as "The Eensy Weensy Spider" or

> Little bird up in a tree, in a tree, in a tree.
> Little bird up in a tree, sing a song to me.
> Sing about the roses on the garden wall;
> Sing about the birdies, in the tree-top tall.
> Sing about the farmer, planting beans and corn,
> Planting peas and carrots, on a summer morn.

ABCs and 123s. We give each parent and child a strip of paper with four pairs of numbers or letters written on it, but mixed up—for example, the strip might have A M C A G C M G. The parent covers each letter or number with a finger, and the child picks a finger for the parent to lift to reveal what's underneath. The child tries to find a match by choosing another finger for the parent to lift. As the child makes matches, the parent tucks fingers in his or her fist. We then sing "Bingo":

> There was a farmer who had a dog,
> and Bingo was his name-O.
> B-I-N-G-O,
> B-I-N-G-O,
> B-I-N-G-O,
> and Bingo was his name.

Each time this verse is repeated, one letter from B-I-N-G-O is dropped and singers clap instead. At the end, everyone claps for all five letters.

Nursery rhymes. Parent-child pairs act out nursery rhymes as the teacher says them out loud. We then sing some of the children's favorite rhymes.

Under the sea. We give each pair a cut-out of an octopus with five tiny fish drawn around the outer edge. Each pair also receives five clothespins with one of the five fish drawn on each one. Children match the pictures, and parents help as they attach the clothespins to the cut-out. We then sing a sea-related song that talks about the children's ages:

> When I was one I ate a bun, going over the sea.
> I jumped aboard a pirate ship, and the pirate said to me:
> Going over, going under, stand at attention, with a 1-2-3.
> When I was two I buckled my shoe...
> When I was three I climbed a tree...
> When I was four I shut the door....

Baby animals at the farm. We have a large barn made of poster board with several cut-out windows, behind each of which is a picture of a full-grown animal. Each parent-child pair is given a set of picture cards of baby animals. Each child takes a turn to open a window, and everyone tries to find the matching baby from the picture cards. We then sing "Old MacDonald Had a Farm."

After the planned activities are over, we finish circle time by asking each child to pick a song for us all to sing together. The children sit on their parents' laps or snuggle up beside them for this, and they try to be close even during the action songs. For example, in "Row, Row, Row Your Boat," a child might sit on a parent's lap, and they can both hold hands to row and rock back and forth as the song gets faster or slower.

These songs and activities are not just for circle time, though. Children enjoy doing these things with their parents at home, and this gives everyone more chances for talking and playing together.

Learning About Playing, Playing While Learning

Following circle time, the parents in our program meet in one room with their teacher while the children are busy in the play room. We call this Parents Together Time, or PTT. It gives the parents a chance to have discussions and work on a variety of projects, including designing play activities. (Many examples of these activities are given in Chapter 3.) At the end of the day, parents and children meet again and try these activities together for about 30 minutes. The parents come to play time ready to be with their children and to try their new ideas, and the children are happy to do something new and to have their parents' attention again.

Besides working on the actual games and activities to do later with their children, during PTT the parents have a chance to talk about the importance of playing. Play is your child's work—it's how he learns about things, including language and literacy. Think about these questions:

- What do you think is the most important skill that the young child has to learn?
- How is it that by the age of 5, before they ever go to school, most children know a lot about how to communicate with adults?
- What has been happening to the child during those 5 years to help him learn how to use language?
- When do parents start talking to their children?
- How much time do you think you spend talking with your child every day?

Play is important for the child. But what can parents do to make sure that play time is fun and successful for everyone? We teach five different strategies parents can keep in mind:

1. *Observe*

   Take time to observe your child's mood, interests, and style of play. Is he nonstop action? Is he a little shy right now? Try to pick up on your child's interests and mood when you start to play.

2. *Approach*

   Join in your child's play slowly, without taking charge or disrupting things. Start talking with him in a way that says you respect what's going on.

3. *Follow your child's lead*

   Be a play partner, but let your child be in charge of the action. Respect his ideas; allow him to create his own ways of playing or pretending.

4. *Extend and expand play*

   Ask questions that help your child experiment with play materials and learn about new things. Say things that describe what he is doing or what the main idea of the activity is supposed to be. But don't go overboard and talk too much instead of playing! Also, avoid being critical. Instead of "No, not that way" try "You made all the blocks fall down. Were they a castle?"

5. *Stay on your child's level*
Use a calm voice and gestures that show him you're there. Encourage him with nods or smiles, and try to keep at eye level with him.

Parents are always interested in their children's ideas. When you take time to relax and really see what's going on when you play with your child, you will soon notice how much your child is learning and how curious and creative he is. We try to help parents in our program keep track of how things go with their children during play time by asking them to fill out the "Let's Observe" form on the next page. Very quickly, though, playing becomes natural for everyone, and the form is no longer needed.

Of course, parents also want to see how their children are growing and developing. A regular play time is a great opportunity to observe gradual changes in children's language, thinking, and social and emotional growth. "Child Observation Checklists," where a teacher or a teacher and parent together note observations about each child at specific times, can let parents in our program see this growth. (Copies of these checklists appear on pages 19 to 21.) When parents look back over the completed checklists, they marvel at how their children use new words, ask different questions, use new social skills with other children, and learn how to express feelings.

In the next chapter, we give step-by-step instructions about activities parents in our program actually designed and tried with their children. We hope that you will be able to use or adapt some of them to fill hours of fun with your own child.

Let's Observe

Parents and Children Playing and Talking

Observing your own talk	Not at all	Sometimes	Often
1. I asked questions to encourage my child to talk.			
2. I used names and labels as I played so my child could imitate me.			
3. I used specific words for color, size, and shape.			
4. I described what my child was doing as we played.			
5. I reminded my child of other related experiences when we played.			

Observing your child's talk My child uses language...	Not at all	Sometimes	Often
1. to request help.			
2. to engage me in play ("You be the...").			
3. to request information ("What ...?").			
4. to plan the next activity or tell me how to play.			
5. to label or name something.			
6. to explain an activity or how a toy works.			

Parents and Children Interacting

During play time, I should remember to...
• show kindness and interest in my child's ideas.
• join in play themes without dominating.
• allow my child to direct the action.
• follow my child's lead by respecting his or her ideas and ability to make decisions.
• look for ways to respond and build on my child's ideas.

For each question, circle the O (often), S (some), or N (never). Then use the blank space to tell something about how you felt about that aspect of your playing together.

1. Do I observe how my child interacts? (For example, did I notice if she was quiet? Excited? Does she want help? Or does she prefer to figure out things alone?)

    O S N

    I felt that _____.

2. Do I approach my child slowly, with respect?

    O S N

    I felt that _____.

3. Do I allow my child to take the lead? Do I follow that lead?

    O S N

    I felt that _____.

4. Do I encourage my child's play by staying involved with his play theme and helping him to discover new directions?

    O S N

    I felt that _____.

5. Do I use gestures, expressions, and a tone of voice to show I support my child and am there?

    O S N

    I felt that _____.

Child Observation Checklists

Note the date at the top of each column, and enter your rating in each box.
1 = not at all
2 = some of the time
3 = most of the time
4 = always

Let's observe: Language

Talk with other children	Date:	Date:	Date:	Notes:
• Withdrawn or ignoring				
• Aware, but does not participate				
• Cooperates				
• Initiates				
• Is directed				
• Directs				
Talk with adult				
• Reluctant				
• Initiates				
• Responds when approached				
• Maintains dialogue with ease				
Characteristics of behavior				
• Quiet/shy/timid				
• Confident/friendly				
• Dominant/aggressive				
• Uses language to focus on the task at hand				
Language use				
• Attempts to imitate words				
• Labels objects independently				
• Uses color words				
• Uses time words				
• Uses quantity words				
• Uses number words				

(continued)

1 = not at all
2 = some of the time
3 = most of the time
4 = always

Let's observe: Play

Free play	Date:	Date:	Date:	Notes:
• Unsettled, distracted, moves quickly from toy to toy				
• Plays alone with selected toys				
• Stays with one activity for a long time				
• Uses toys for make believe				
• Plans and builds with toys				
• Plays with another child but does "own thing"				
• Shares, takes turns				
• Makes play plans with another child				
Small-group play (adult led)				
• Disinterested, distracted				
• Watches but does not join in				
• Follows a one-step direction				
• Follows two-step directions				
• Attempts activity with little supervision				
• Shares, takes turns				
• Adds own ideas				
Characteristics of play				
• Sings, laughs, claps, etc.				
• Strong sense of "mine" (grabs, pushes, etc.)				
• Uses a physical defense of "play rights"				
• Asks for help when needed				
• Talks while playing				
• Settles conflicts with adult help				
• Initiates constructive solutions to conflicts				

(continued)

1 = not at all
2 = beginning
3 = consolidating
4 = mastery

Let's observe: Intellectual and physical development

Cognitive abilities	Date:	Date:	Date:	Notes:
• Understands comparative words (*more than*, *less than*, *bigger*, *smaller*, etc.)				
• Uses time concepts (tomorrow, today, yesterday)				
• Knows days of the week.				
• Sorts by: shape size color				
• Relates numerals to quantities				
• Counts to 5				
• Counts to 10				
• Points to and names two to four colors				
• Points to and names four to six colors				
• Can pair associated objects or pictures				
• Draws a person with two to six recognizable parts				
• Names and matches parts drawn to own body				
Motor skills				
• Can manipulate writing/drawing instruments				
• Cuts with scissors				
• Shows awareness of personal space				
• Shows gross motor coordination: moves without bumping into things or people rides tricycle climbs				
Mastery motivation				
• Persistent when problems are encountered				
• "Keeps head" emotionally when frustrated or in difficulty				
• Thoughtful—is reflective or considered in approach to problems				

Chapter 3

Activities to Do Together

Parents and children both say that one of their favorite parts of our family literacy program is Make-Try-Take. We call it this because parents *make* the activity in Parents Together Time, *try* the activity with their children at play time, and then *take* it home to use. Each week there are four activities, all related to a theme. Usually a pair of parents in the group is responsible for coming up with ideas for the week's activities, and all the parents put them together on Monday during PTT. Each day, one activity is done with the children later in the play room. (Friday is our "catch-up" day, so there are no special play activities on that day.)

Children and parents experiment, discover, and learn with Make-Try-Take. But most important, doing the activities gives the parents time to be with their children, to do things together, to show them how much they love them, and to let them know what a great job they're doing. And this goes on even further, because the activities can be played with over and over again outside of school. They are all made from simple materials that are easy to find, and most of them require only a little preparation. Parents and children can expand the activities and invent new games to include items and areas in their homes. Other family members usually get involved, too. Parents enjoy changing the activities so they can be done with their older and younger children. All this gives parents and children new ways to spend time together—playing, learning, sharing, and helping each other.

As mentioned earlier, in our program the activities each week are organized around a theme. We try to pick these to match things that are happening outside of school—so, in October we might be thinking about harvesting fruit and vegetables or dressing up for Halloween, and in the spring our themes could be baby animals or how plants grow. We also try to start each new term with themes and activities that are fairly simple or that teach basic skills such as recognizing shapes or colors. We then work up to more complex themes, such as "Imagination Zone" or "Under the Sea."

One of the things that is most important in choosing themes and activities, though, is to think about all the different things children may learn by doing them. Children develop in three key areas: social/emotional, language/intellectual, and physical. The "Parent Guide to Children's Learning" (page 24) lists action words that relate to these areas. If parents check with this guide when they are making up activities to do with their children, they will be able to make sure to touch on these important aspects of learning.

In order to keep track of what sort of learning the activities may promote, parents in our program use Make-Try-Take activity guides. These sheets tell what learning areas are the focus, and give instructions about how to do each activity. There is also space in the "Talking With My Child" section where parents can write how they talked when they were playing together, what their child says about the activity, and what learning went on. In our program, parents also rate the week's four activities (1 is the activity most liked by the child and 4 is the least) and give a reason for the rating. Parents also could use this space to write whether their child thought the activity was excellent, good, OK, or not too much fun, and give reasons or ideas of how it could be improved. Even not-so-successful activities have a positive side: It might be that doing the activity teaches you that your child

Parent Guide to Children's Learning

Children learn language by...

imitating sounds
singing songs
making rhymes
asking and answering questions
listening
explaining
doing finger plays
pretending
explaining their ideas
describing things
comparing things
telling stories
sharing books
labeling
following directions
describing patterns
playing make-believe

Children learn about math, space, and time by...

sorting things
talking about the time of day
putting things in order
counting
grouping things
drawing and labeling shapes
talking about more and less
matching things
making patterns
creating charts and graphs
talking about above and below, under and over, on top of, underneath, and beside
recognizing numbers
doing puzzles

Children develop fine motor skills by...

gluing
lacing
drawing
tracing
cutting
stacking
tearing
sewing

Children develop gross motor skills by...

jumping
running
twisting
climbing
walking
throwing and catching
skipping
balancing
bending
bouncing a ball

Children learn social skills by...

sharing
taking turns
pretending together
talking together
cooperating
helping one another
expressing their feelings

Children develop thinking skills by...

completing patterns
pretending
using their senses
playing memory games
doing puzzles
sorting things
noting similarities and differences
dramatizing
answering "what if" questions

doesn't really like puzzles, that she isn't ready for learning about spelling, or that she already knows how to count to 10.

Whether you are designing activities to do with your child in a program like ours or on your own at home, the "Activity Planning Guide" will probably be helpful. It contains reminders for getting play materials together and about ways to talk with your child while you are playing and learning together. As you become more comfortable with these sorts of activities, you will find it easy to come up with new ideas for them. Sometimes a visit from a relative, something your child finds, or a question your child asks will give you an idea for a new activity. There are also a number of good resources for parents and teachers that give ideas for meaningful activities. Some recommended titles appear in the "Extra Resources" list on the next page.

Activity Planning Guide

Prepare activities according to a theme. Think about how you will do each activity with your child:

1. What materials do I need for the activity?
2. What parts will I do?
3. What parts will my child do? Does the activity match my child's level of learning and interest? If it doesn't, how can I change it?
4. Does the activity encourage talking with my child? What questions could I ask that involve more than a yes or no answer? What might I tell my child that would be interesting to her? How can I encourage my child to ask me questions? What actions or sounds can we do? How many of our senses can we use?

Helpful hints:
• Find a quiet spot away from others.
• Do not force your child to do the activity. If he is tired or wants to show you something else, try the activity later.
• Let your child do as much as possible by herself.
• Praise your child sincerely and often. Say things like "I love your picture!"
• Ask your child questions that you thought of before you started the activity.
• Be patient. Understanding of routines, attention span, interests, and motor skills will develop. Remember—it is not the final product that is important, it is the process that counts.
• Feel good about yourself and what you are doing.
• Have fun and enjoy your child. She is terrific!
• *Most important*: Listen to your child. Encourage him or her to expand comments and answers by asking "thinking" questions (who, what, where, when, why, how).

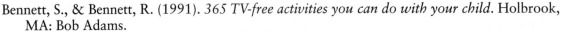

Bennett, S., & Bennett, R. (1991). *365 TV-free activities you can do with your child*. Holbrook, MA: Bob Adams.

Clancy, L. (1991). *Preschool teacher's month by month activities program*. West Nyack, NY: Center for Applied Research in Education.

Claycomb, P. (1992). *The busy classroom*. Mt. Rainier, MD: Gryphon House.

Croft, D. (1990). *Activities handbook for teachers of young children* (5th ed.). Boston, MA: Houghton Mifflin.

Forte, I. (1988). *The early childhood teacher's every-day-all-year-long book of units, activities, and patterns*. Nashville, TN: Incentive Publications.

Frank, M. (1976). *I can make a rainbow*. Nashville, TN: Incentive Publications.

Galloway, L., Ivey, G., & Valster, R. (1990). *Daily plans for active preschoolers*. West Nyack, NY: Center for Applied Research in Education.

Green, M. (1995). *Teaching from cupboards and closets*. Glenview, IL: Goodyear.

Hanna, S., & Wilford, S. (1990). *Floor time: Tuning in to each child* [Video and guide]. New York: Scholastic.

Herr, J., & Libby, Y. (1990). *Designing creative materials for young children*. New York: Harcourt Brace Jovanovich.

Kohl, M.F. (1985). *Scribble cookies and other independent creative art experiences for children*. Bellingham, WA: Bright Ring.

Mailbox Magazine—Preschool. Greensboro, NC: Educational Center.

Warren, J. (1985). *1•2•3 Art*. Everett, WA: Totline.

Warren, J.(1989). *Theme-a-saurus*. Everett, WA: Totline.

Warren, J. (1991). *Alphabet theme-a-saurus*. Everett, WA: Totline.

Wilmes, L., & Wilmes, D. (1990). *Make-take games*. Elgin, IL: Building Blocks.

Following are examples of activity guides made by parents in our program for some of our themes. We hope that they will get you started on hours of fun and learning with your child.

Me, Myself, and I

My Hands and Feet

Importance: developing motor skills, differentiating sizes

Materials: large sheet of paper; marker, crayon, pencil, or pen

Here's how:

1. Draw a line down the center of the paper.
2. At the top of one section print, " [your child's name] 's hands and feet." In the other section print "Mom's [or Dad's] hands and feet.
3. Either you or your child traces the hands and feet onto the paper.

Talking with my child: _____

_____

_____

_____

Rank: _____

Why? _____

_____

Body Images

Importance: developing fine motor skills, labeling, connecting words and the objects they represent, expressing creativity, representing something on paper

Materials: sheet of paper larger than your child, markers, crayons, pencils

Here's how:

1. Have your child carefully lie down on the paper.
2. Trace your child's body shape with a pencil.
3. You and your child can now color the body, adding whatever you feel like in terms of face, hair, clothes, etc.

Variation: Use yarn or string to outline the body, then fill in the outline with real clothes and make a face with marbles for eyes, a banana for a mouth, etc.

Talking with my child: _____

_____

_____

_____

Rank: _____
Why? _____

_____

Laundry Bag

Importance: labeling, matching, recognizing shapes

Materials: construction paper; scissors; large paper bag; markers, crayons, or pencils

Here's how:

1. Cut the construction paper into shapes of clothing such as shirts, pants, and socks, and put the cut-outs in the paper bag.
2. Have your child reach in and pull out one shape. Ask your child to name the piece of clothing and tell what part of the body it is worn on.

Variations:

1. Using children's scissors, your child can help cut out the shapes. She could also draw pictures of clothes on the bag.
2. Put real clothes in the bag. Have your child close her eyes before pulling out something, and ask her to try to figure out what the item is without looking.

Talking with my child: _____

_____

_____

_____

Rank: _____
Why? _____

_____

"This Is Me" Poster

Importance: recognizing different aspects of self, developing self-esteem and self-confidence, connecting spoken with written words, improving comprehension

Materials: photograph of your child, sheet of 11″ x 14″ (27.5 cm x 35 cm) paper, marker or pen, tape or glue

Here's how:

1. Glue or tape the photograph to the paper and print your child's name near it.

2. Decide on some things that you would like your child to tell about himself, making a draft of ideas such as "how he looks," "what he likes to do," "what he likes to eat," and so on.

3. Using these ideas, think of sentences that relate to them. Print these on the poster, but leave a blank space where your child can fill in a missing word. For example, you might write, "My hair is _____," "I love to eat _____," and "_____ is my favorite toy."

4. Read the sentences with your child and have him say the missing word. You or your child print the word in the space. Encourage your child to add his own sentences.

5. Decorate the poster with coloring, stamps, collage, etc.

Variation: Play a "Finish My Sentence" game. You or your child say a sentence, but leave out a word. The other person tries to fill in the missing word.

Talking with my child: _____

_____

_____

_____

Rank: _____

Why? _____

_____

School Fun

So Many School Buses!

Importance: developing fine motor skills, counting

Materials: plain paper, sponges, yellow paint, paint tray, scissors, construction paper

Here's how:

1. Draw a picture of a school bus or trace one from a children's book. Cut out the shape to make a paper pattern. Stick the pattern on a sponge, and use it to cut the sponge into a school bus shape.

2. Pour some paint into a flat dish, such as a the throw-away tray from a microwave meal.

3. Show your child how to dip the sponge in the paint and press it on the construction paper. Ask her to make as many buses as she'd like, and then count them together.

Talking with my child: _____

_____

_____

_____

Rank: _____

Why? _____

_____

School Book

Importance: developing fine motor skills, connecting spoken and written words, developing self-confidence and pride in accomplishments

Materials: several sheets of plain paper, one sheet of construction paper, stapler, markers or crayons, pen or pencil

Here's how:

1. Cut the sheets of white paper in half widthwise. (Four or five sheets will be enough for most young children.) Stack them neatly, making sure the edges are aligned.

2. Cut the construction paper the same size as the white sheets, and place it on the top of the stack. Fold the whole stack in half widthwise.

3. Staple the papers together at the fold to make a book with the construction paper as its cover.

4. Have your child show and describe to you some of her favorite things from your family literacy program, day care, preschool, or play group—perhaps a toy, teacher, or special friend.

5. Together with your child, think of a sentence about each item or person. Print each sentence on its own page as your child watches. Leave space for him to draw a picture of or about that thing.

6. Ask your child to give the book a title and decorate its cover.

7. Read and reread the book with your child.

Talking with my child: _____

_____

_____

_____

Rank: _____

Why? _____

_____

Hide-and-Seek Puzzle

Importance: developing fine motor skills, problem solving, listening, following directions, matching, identifying visual relationships

Materials: large sheet of stiff paper, markers, scissors

Here's how:

1. Draw a picture about you, your child, and family literacy. Choose something your child likes, such as walking to the building where you attend a program, or a picture of the local library.

2. Cut the picture into pieces. Depending on your child's age and developmental stage, you can make several small pieces with complicated shapes or just a few larger pieces.

3. Practice putting the puzzle together with your child a few times.

4. Now ask your child to close her eyes and count to 10 or say the alphabet while you hide the puzzle pieces around the room.

5. Have your child find the pieces by following clues—for example, if you hid a piece in a pot, you might say "It's inside something Dad cooks with." You can let your child know that she's getting close to a piece by saying, "You're getting warmer," and if

she gets too far off track, you can give her directions like "Take five big steps straight ahead."

6. Put the puzzle together again once she's found all the pieces.

Variation: Hide the pieces from a ready-made puzzle you may have at home.

Talking with my child: _____

_____

_____

_____

Rank: _____

Why? _____

_____

Our Spectacular Senses

Binoculars

Importance: developing fine motor skills, using sense of sight, listening, problem solving

Materials: cardboard tubes from two toilet paper rolls, string, stickers, markers, stapler, tape

Here's how:

1. Staple or tape the rolls together (long sides touching) so they look like binoculars.
2. Attach a string to the rolls so they will hang around your child's neck.
3. Suggest to your child that she color the binoculars and decorate them with stickers.
4. Teach your child to play "I Spy." She looks around the room with her binoculars, secretly picks an object, and then uses a clue to describe it ("I spy with my little eye something that is..."). You try to guess what she's spying.
5. Take turns using the binoculars and finding something to "spy."

Variation: Use make-believe binoculars by cupping your hands around your eyes.

Talking with my child: _____

_____

_____

_____

Rank: _____
Why? _____

_____

Touch Cards

Importance: developing language skills for describing, using sense of touch

Materials: several index cards (or a large sheet of stiff paper), items with various textures (pipe cleaners, tin foil, sandpaper, bubble wrap, small pieces of different types of fabric such as velvet or corduroy), glue or tape

Here's how:

1. If you don't have index cards, cut some 3″ x 5″ (7.5 cm x 12.5 cm) cards from the stiff paper.

2. Attach one of the items from your collection of texture materials to each card.

3. Ask your child to close his eyes and feel one card at a time. Ask him to describe how each card feels.

Variation: Ask your child to close his eyes, and then guide him to different things in the house—maybe a pillow on the couch or a furry jacket that he can touch and describe.

Talking with my child: _____

_____

_____

_____

Rank: _____

Why? _____

_____

Scented Cups

Importance: developing language skills for describing, using sense of smell

Materials: small paper cups, cotton balls, samples of things that have different and distinctive scents (perfume, vanilla, cinnamon, dirt, etc.)

Here's how:

1. Put enough of each scented item in a paper cup so it can be smelled easily, or dab a little of the liquid "scents" on cotton balls.

2. Ask your child to smell each item and describe the scents.

Talking with my child: _____

_____

_____

_____

Rank: _____

Why? _____

_____

Frantic Faces

Importance: developing gross motor skills, using sense of hearing (listening to differentiate sounds), understanding concepts (slower/faster, louder/softer)

Materials: two sturdy paper plates; popcorn (unpopped) or rice; stapler or tape; markers, stamps, stickers, etc.

Here's how:

1. Ask your child to decorate the paper plates or draw faces on them.
2. Sprinkle some popcorn or rice on one plate, and staple or tape the other on top.
3. Ask your child to shake the "plate rattle." How would you shake it if the face were mad? Sad? Happy? Tired?

Variation: Fill child-safe containers (plastic bottles or food-storage containers, for example) with different things such as popcorn, macaroni, rice, or flour. Ask your child to describe the sound made by shaking each one.

Talking with my child: _____

_____

_____

_____

Rank: _____

Why? _____

_____

Transportation

Making Tracks

Importance: developing fine motor skills, understanding cause and effect

Materials: paint; paper; toy cars, trucks, or anything with wheels
Here's how:

1. Pour some paint into a large, flat dish or onto a plate.
2. Have your child carefully dip the toy car or truck into the paint and then "drive" it on the paper to make tracks.

Variation: Suggest that your child drive her tricycle through puddles or mud and then onto a dry sidewalk or driveway.

Talking with my child: _____

_____

_____

_____

Rank: _____
Why? _____

_____

How Do You Get There?

Importance: understanding concepts (distances), learning about categories (different modes of transportation), problem solving

Materials: a brass fastener, a sheet of drawing paper, a sheet of stiff paper such as heavy construction paper or poster board, scissors
Here's how:

1. Cut a circle about 8″ (20 cm) in diameter out of the drawing paper. Cut a circle about 9″ (22.5 cm) in diameter and an arrow about 3″ (7.5 cm) long out of the stiff paper.
2. Draw lines on the drawing paper circle to divide it into pie sections (as many as you want).
3. In each piece of the pie draw (or trace) a mode of transportation that your child is familiar with: feet, bike, car, boat, plane, in-line skates, bus, etc.

4. Glue or tape the picture circle to the larger circle. Place the arrow at the center and poke the brass fastener through all pieces, and then flatten the fastener at the back.

5. Ask your child how you get to a certain destination—for example, "How do you get to visit Grandma?" or "How do you get to the grocery store?" The child turns the arrow to point to the mode of transportation and names it.

6. Switch roles with your child so that he asks the questions and you point the arrow.

Variation: Tell your child to pretend that different parts of your home are different locations—a bedroom might be the local convenience store, the sofa an island, and so on. Ask him to pretend to be the kind of transportation he would use to get from one location to another. He could stretch out his arms to be an airplane, for example.

Talking with my child: _____

_____

_____

_____

Rank: _____

Why? _____

_____

Magnetic Motion

Importance: understanding concepts (transportation, magnetism)

Materials: drawing paper; construction paper; magnets; glue or tape; pen, pencils, or markers

Here's how:

1. Draw a scene that includes roads, the sky, and water.

2. Draw cars, buses, ships, planes, etc., on the construction paper and cut them out.

3. Attach a small magnet to the back of each cut-out. Attach the cut-outs to the scene by placing another magnet behind each one on the other side of the paper, but don't attach this second magnet to the paper.

4. With your child, move the cut-outs through your scene by moving the magnets on the back. Make up a story about where everyone is going as you play.

Variation: Use refrigerator magnets and a paper scene on the fridge.

Talking with my child: _____

_____

_____

_____

Rank: _____

Why? _____

_____

Match 'Em

Importance: matching, problem solving

Materials: index cards (or stiff paper); scissors; markers, colored pencils, or crayons

Here's how:

1. If you don't have index cards, cut out an even number of 3″ x 5″ (7.5 cm x 12.5 cm) cards from the drawing paper.
2. Take two cards. On one draw a type of transportation (such as a boat) and on the other draw a simple scene where it might appear (such as water).
3. Repeat step 2 until you have the number of pairs you would like.
4. Mix up the cards, and ask your child to match them.

Talking with my child: _____

_____

_____

_____

Rank: _____

Why? _____

_____

ABCs and 123s

Catching Raindrops

Importance: developing gross motor skills, counting, understanding one-to-one correspondence

Materials: construction paper (one sheet blue and one sheet another color), scissors

Here's how:

1. Cut out several small raindrops from the blue paper and a fairly large umbrella shape from the other paper.
2. Gently toss raindrops in the air so that your child can try to catch them on the umbrella. Together count the raindrops he caught.
3. Play again, switching roles.

Variation: Use a plastic dish or bowl and pennies instead of the umbrella and raindrops.

Talking with my child: _____
_____
_____
_____

Rank: _____
Why? _____
_____

Match the Numbers

Importance: recognizing numbers, understanding one-to-one correspondence, matching

Materials: index cards (or stiff paper), scissors, markers, stickers

Here's how:

1. If you don't have index cards, cut construction paper into 3" x 5" (7.5 cm x 12.5 cm) cards.
2. Print a number on one side of each card and draw that number of dots (or stick on that number of stickers) on the other side.
3. Cut the cards in half, and mix up the pieces.

4. With your child, match the dot cards with the corresponding number cards.

Variation: Point out the date on a calendar. Together, find that number of things of one type, and write down on the calendar square what you found.

Talking with my child: _____
_____
_____
_____

Rank: _____
Why? _____
_____

Connect the Dots

Importance: developing fine motor skills, recognizing given name, recognizing letters

Materials: large piece of paper, markers

Here's how:

1. Spell out your child's name in large, well-spaced dots on the paper.
2. With your child, connect the dots so that she recognizes the letters one by one and "writes" her name.

Variation: Trace letters and numbers in the newspaper or in magazines.

Talking with my child: _____
_____
_____
_____

Rank: _____
Why? _____
_____

The Best Alphabet Book

Importance: recognizing letters, connecting spoken and written words, building self-confidence and self-esteem

Materials: several sheets of plain paper, stapler, glue or tape, construction paper, scissors, collection of old magazines or catalogs

Here's how:

1. Stack the sheets of paper and fold in half widthwise. Staple along the fold to make a book.

2. Cut out a set of letters from the construction paper. In the old magazines, find a picture of an object that begins with each letter and cut it out. (For hard-to-match letters, you can draw a picture or find something in the magazines that contains the letter, as long as its sound is heard.)

3. Ask your child to match the letters and pictures.

4. Glue each match into your alphabet book.

5. Let your child read the book to you.

Talking with my child: _____
_____
_____
_____

Rank: _____
Why? _____
_____

1-2-3 Ladybug

Importance: recognizing numbers, counting, understanding one-to-one correspondence, matching

Materials: green poster board, red construction paper, black markers, glue, scissors

Here's how:

1. Draw a large, simple leaf shape on the green board. Cut it out.

2. Cut out twenty 4″ circles from the red paper. These will be the basic shape for ladybugs.

3. Divide the circles into two groups of ten. Draw one dot on one circle from each group, two dots on a circle from each group, and so on through ten dots. Add facial features to each of the "bugs."

4. Glue one set of ladybugs to the large leaf in random order.

5. Cut out a square of construction paper to make a pocket, and glue it to the back of the leaf. Put the second set of ladybugs in the pocket.

6. Show the leaf to your child. Ask him to take the ladybugs out of the pocket and spread them out near the leaf.

7. He should then pick up one ladybug, count the spots, and find the matching bug on the leaf.

8. Continue counting dots and matching ladybugs until each one has a twin.

Talking with my child: _____

_____

_____

_____

Rank: _____

Why? _____

_____

Nursery Rhymes

Coloring Book

Importance: connecting written and spoken words, recognizing written words, representing words with images, developing fine motor skills

Materials: photocopies of nursery rhymes taken from children's books, two sheets of construction paper, markers

Here's how:

1. Choose several rhymes and staple them together to make a book, with construction paper for the front and back covers.
2. With your child, draw pictures—around the rhymes if there's room or on the back of each page—to illustrate the rhymes.
3. Recite the rhymes with your child.

Variations:

1. If the rhymes you've photocopied are already illustrated, ask your child to color in the pictures.
2. If you can't find good rhymes to photocopy, print some rhymes that you know on blank paper to make the book's pages.

Talking with my child: _____
_____
_____
_____

Rank: _____
Why? _____
_____

Rebus Nursery Rhyme

Importance: connecting images with written and spoken words, recognizing written words

Materials: collection of old magazines or catalogs, scissors, marker, sheet of large paper, tape or glue

Here's how:

1. Choose a nursery rhyme that your child likes.

2. Flip through the magazines and catalogs looking for pictures of things mentioned in the nursery rhyme. For example, if you chose "Mary Had a Little Lamb," you might find pictures of a little girl, a lamb, and snow. Cut out the pictures or photocopy them.

3. Print the nursery rhyme on large paper. When you come to one of the words you have a picture for, glue or tape the picture in that spot instead of writing the word. Substitute as many pictures for words as possible—if you couldn't find too many pictures, try drawing some.

4. Ask you child to read the rhyme with you. Encourage her to read as much as possible on her own.

Talking with my child: _____

_____

_____

_____

Rank: _____

Why? _____

_____

Tube Puppets

Importance: dramatizing, learning about story, practicing oral language

Materials: several tubes from paper towel rolls; pictures of people, animals, or other "characters" cut out from magazines or photocopied from books; glue or tape

Here's how:

1. Choose a nursery rhyme. Find pictures from your collection that match the characters mentioned. For example, if you choose "Hey Diddle Diddle," you'll need a cat, a cow, a dog, a dish, and a spoon.

2. If necessary, draw or color on the pictures—maybe adding a fiddle to the cat cut-out, for instance. Attach the figures to tubes.

3. Use the tube puppets with your child to act out the nursery rhyme as you recite it together.

Talking with my child: _____

_____

_____

_____

Rank: _____

Why? _____

_____

Magical Mobile

Importance: developing fine motor skills, practicing oral language

Materials: coat hanger, pieces of string or yarn of varying lengths, scissors, glue, drawings or photocopies of nursery rhyme characters (two of each)

Here's how:

1. Cut out the characters.
2. Glue a piece of string to the back of one of each pair, then glue the back of the second of the pair to the back of the first. Repeat this until you have five or six characters.
3. Ask your child to color the characters.
4. Use the strings to tie the characters to the coat hanger to make a mobile.
5. Recite the matching nursery rhymes together.

Talking with my child: _____

_____

_____

_____

Rank: _____

Why? _____

_____

Shapes and Colors

Colorful Coffee Filters

Importance: developing fine motor skills, recognizing colors, imagining

Materials: paper coffee filters; watered-down paint or food coloring dissolved in water; eye dropper, straw, or spoon

Here's how:

1. Show your child how to use the eye dropper, spoon, or straw to get a few drops of the paint or colored water.

2. Have your child drop the water onto the coffee filter.

3. Together, try to recognize shapes or figures in the spreading colors, in the same way you can sometimes imagine things when you look at the shapes of clouds. Talk about the colors and name them.

Talking with my child: _____

_____

_____

_____

Rank: _____

Why? _____

_____

Paint Cans

Importance: developing fine motor skills, recognizing colors, memorizing

Materials: drawing paper, scissors, markers or crayons

Here's how:

1. Draw several paint cans (or draw one and photocopy it). For a young child, eight or ten should be enough.

2. Ask your child to color the cans, making sure he does at least two in each color.

3. Cut out the cans.

4. Turn the cans color-side down on a table.

5. Play a memory game with your child. First, you turn over two cans, trying to find a match of colors. If the two don't match, turn them both color-side down again; if they do match, name the color and put the cans in front of you. Then your child takes a turn.

6. Keep taking turns until all the cans are matched.

Talking with my child: _____

_____

_____

_____

Rank: _____

Why? _____

_____

Bag of Color

Importance: recognizing colors, learning about color mixing

Materials: plastic bag that can be sealed, spoon, a few colors of fingerpaint, paper

Here's how:

1. Spoon one color of paint into the bag and seal it firmly. Have your child spread it around.

2. Spoon another color of paint into the bag and seal it firmly. Have your child mix the two colors together.

3. Repeat step 2 as many times as desired.

4. Open the bag and let your child fingerpaint with the color she made herself.

Talking with my child: _____

_____

_____

_____

Rank: _____

Why? _____

_____

Pizza Party

Importance: recognizing colors, recognizing shapes

Materials: stiff paper or poster board, colored paper, scissors, glue, a marker or crayon

Here's how:

1. Cut a large circle out of the stiff paper. With a marker, divide it into six "slices of pizza."

2. Using construction paper, cut out pizza-topping shapes: six red triangles (slightly smaller than the slices) for the sauce, several brown circles for pepperoni, green strips for the green pepper, yellow squares for pineapple chunks, etc.

3. Make a pizza with your child, naming the shapes and colors as you go along.

Talking with my child: _____

_____

_____

_____

Rank: _____

Why? _____

_____

Shape Person

Importance: labeling, recognizing shapes

Materials: construction paper, scissors, glue

Here's how:

1. Working together, cut out shapes to make a person—circles of various sizes for the head and eyes; a square, rectangle, or oval for the body; long, skinny rectangles for arms and legs; a small crescent for the mouth, etc.

2. Glue the shape person together on a sheet of paper, naming the shapes and body parts as you go along.

Variations:

1. Arrange the shape person on a table or paper, but don't glue the pieces down. Once your child is familiar with it, he can use the pieces again and again as a puzzle.

2. Cut out shapes to make a house, dog, cat, etc.

Talking with my child: _____

_____

_____

_____

Rank: _____

Why? _____

_____

Shape Twister

Importance: recognizing shapes, following directions, developing gross motor skills

Materials: sheet of poster board or other large paper, markers

Here's how:

1. Draw three to five shapes on the large paper. You may want to include shapes of things, such as an umbrella, a snowman, or a house, along with "regular" shapes such as circles or triangles.

2. Put the paper down on the floor.

3. You and your child both take off your shoes.

4. Take turns giving and following directions. For example, you could start by saying, "Put your hand on the triangle" or "Touch the house with your foot." After doing the action, your child might tell you to "Jump up and down on the circle."

Talking with my child: _____

_____

_____

_____

Rank: _____

Why? _____

_____

Color Wheel

Importance: recognizing colors, matching

Materials: brass fastener, six different colors of construction paper, scissors, glue, stiff paper, paper plate, marker

Here's how:

1. With a marker, divide the plate into six sections (like slices of pizza). Cut out triangles of the same size as the slices from each of the sheets of construction paper. Glue the construction paper triangles onto each of the segments on the paper plate.

2. Cut an arrow shape out of the stiff paper and fasten it to the middle of the plate with a brass fastener. You should be able to spin it around so that it points at the different colored segments on the paper plate.

3. From the scraps of construction paper, cut out a few different shapes.

4. Ask your child to spin the arrow. When it stops, he should find a shape that matches the color the arrow is pointing to.

Talking with my child: _____

_____

_____

_____

Rank: _____

Why? _____

_____

Under the Sea

Go Fish Game

Importance: recognizing colors, following directions, developing fine motor skills

Materials: large box, blue construction paper, poster board or other stiff paper, four or five different colored markers, glue, scissors, hole punch, string, stick, large paperclip

Here's how:

1. Cover the top of the box with blue construction paper. Cut four or five small slits through the construction paper. Cut out waves from the blue paper and glue them to the sides of the box.

2. Cut out small fish shapes from the poster board. Color each fish a different color. Punch a hole in the top of each one. Stick each fish in one of the slits in the box, so that the top with the hole sticks out but the rest of the fish is hidden under the paper.

3. Tie a piece of string to the stick to make a fishing pole. The hook is a bent paperclip.

4. Tell your child that she's going fishing. Ask her to catch a fish of a certain color.

5. Take turns so she can tell you what color of fish to catch.

Talking with my child: _____
_____
_____
_____

Rank: _____
Why? _____
_____

Handprint Octopus

Importance: recognizing colors, counting, developing fine motor skills

Materials: black construction paper, a few different bright colors of paint, paintbrush, markers

Here's how:

1. Paint your child's palm with one color. Have him use his palm as a stamp by placing it firmly down on the sheet of black paper. This shape makes the octopus's body.

2. Paint one of his fingers with a different color. Have him press his finger down near the palm shape to make one of the octopus's tentacles.

3. Repeat step 2 until the octopus has eight tentacles of various colors.

4. Make the octopus face with markers.

Talking with my child: _____

_____

_____

_____

Rank: _____

Why? _____

_____

Under the Sea Book

Importance: learning about concepts (underwater life), connecting written and spoken words, imagining

Materials: plain paper, construction paper, collection of old magazines or catalogs, stapler, scissors, glue, markers

Here's how:

1. Make a book by stapling construction paper to the top and bottom of a stack of several sheets of white paper.

2. With your child, find pictures of "water things" (fish, coral, swimmers, scuba divers, sunken treasure chests, etc.) to cut out from magazines or catalogs, or color a few pictures yourselves.

3. Glue the pictures into the book to make "Under the Sea" scenes.

4. Ask your child to describe the pictures and scenes. Print what she says on each page.

Talking with my child: _____

_____

_____

_____

Rank: _____

Why? _____

_____

Green and Growing

Gardener's Grab Bag

Importance: labeling, using sense of touch, understanding concepts (plant life)

Materials: gardening tools, seeds, bag

Here's how:

1. Collect several gardening tools, seed packets, and other gardening-related items to put in the bag.
2. Have your child reach in the bag and describe or identify the items he picks before he pulls it out of the bag.
3. If your child isn't sure about something he picks, talk to him about how the item is used in gardening and how it contributes to helping plants grow.

Talking with my child: _____
_____
_____
_____

Rank: _____

Why? _____
_____

Here It Grows

Importance: sorting, understanding a concept (plant life)

Materials: paper; pencils, crayons, or markers; scissors

Here's how:

1. Cut several squares of paper, about 4″ x 4″ (10 cm x 10 cm).
2. On each card draw a different stage of a plant's life: seed, seed with sprout beneath soil, sprout coming through soil, plant, plant with leaves, plant with bud, plant with flower. Do as many or as few of the stages as you like and that you think your child can understand.
4. Mix up the cards and then put them face up on a table.
5. Ask your child to put the cards in order.

Variation: For younger children, simply draw a plant with an increasing number of leaves. They may find it easier to put the cards in order according to the number of leaves, rather than following the life cycle.

Talking with my child: _____

_____

_____

_____

Rank: _____

Why? _____

_____

Measure the Plant

Importance: recognizing numbers, making comparisons, measuring
Materials: paper, markers, scissors, rulers, glue
Here's how:

1. Cut several pieces of paper of varying sizes.
2. On each piece, draw a plant of a different height.
3. On a separate paper print the measurement of each plant—for example, 4 inches, 8 centimeters, and so on. Cut out each number.
4. Measure each plant with your child and ask him to tell you what the number on the ruler is.
5. Ask him to find the matching cut-out number and glue it to the plant picture.

Talking with my child: _____

_____

_____

_____

Rank: _____

Why? _____

_____

Chapter 4

Family Reading Time

Reading with young children takes you into a wonderful world. This is a special time, a time to share old favorites and make new discoveries together. In fact, the most important part of shared reading is not the words in the book—it is simply taking the time to be with your child. It may be only a few minutes spent looking at the pictures in a book, but the experience of doing something together builds a positive relationship between parent and child, and it lays the foundation for a lifelong love of reading.

The experts have shown again and again that reading with young children does help them when they begin school. But even though reading is so important in so many ways, making time for it can be difficult. Parents are busy and have many daily demands on them. In addition, not all adults have happy childhood memories of reading, and many (if not most) don't know where to begin in finding books to share and ways to share them. Thinking about your own experiences can help, even if they were negative. In addition to recalling your own reading with your parents or other adults, remembering what you liked best, how family reading made you feel, and what you would do differently with your own children can help you clarify your expectations about reading at home with your children.

When you are first thinking about making a commitment to family reading, there are a few questions to consider:

- What do you see as the benefits and downsides of reading time together?

- When you have shared a book with your child, did he reach out to you or snuggle in closer? What were your feelings as you read to your child? How do you think he felt?

- What are some reasons it may be hard to find time each day to read with your child? Is there anything you can do to change this?

- Of all the things you like to do with your child, how do you rate reading?

Besides thinking about these questions, parents in our family literacy program complete the "Reading With Young Children" survey. This provides another way to review opinions about and experiences of reading with children. When encouraged to reflect in this way, most parents begin to realize why they think about reading the way they do and to understand how certain practices have developed in their families. They also start to see how they might be able to change things to make reading a bigger part of their everyday routines.

Children's Books and Strategies for Family Reading

Each week in the Family Learning Program we have sessions to talk about children's books and the different things that readers can do to understand what they read. We usually focus on one book for toddlers and one for a school-age child. Thus, each week parents get acquainted with different kinds of children's literature that they can share with their children throughout the primary grades. Parents also can borrow books from our class library to read with their children at home, and we make sure they all know about the wonderful books they can get from the public library. In addition, parents write book re-

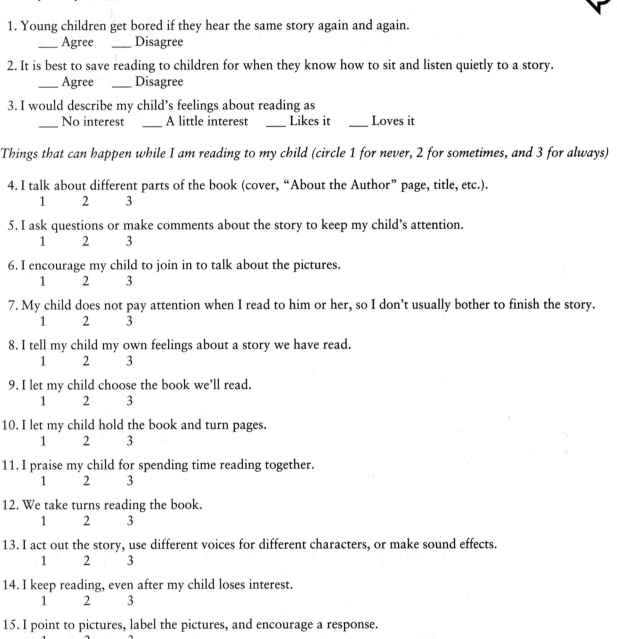

Reading With Young Children

Check your opinion

1. Young children get bored if they hear the same story again and again.
   ___ Agree   ___ Disagree

2. It is best to save reading to children for when they know how to sit and listen quietly to a story.
   ___ Agree   ___ Disagree

3. I would describe my child's feelings about reading as
   ___ No interest   ___ A little interest   ___ Likes it   ___ Loves it

Things that can happen while I am reading to my child (circle 1 for never, 2 for sometimes, and 3 for always)

4. I talk about different parts of the book (cover, "About the Author" page, title, etc.).
   1   2   3

5. I ask questions or make comments about the story to keep my child's attention.
   1   2   3

6. I encourage my child to join in to talk about the pictures.
   1   2   3

7. My child does not pay attention when I read to him or her, so I don't usually bother to finish the story.
   1   2   3

8. I tell my child my own feelings about a story we have read.
   1   2   3

9. I let my child choose the book we'll read.
   1   2   3

10. I let my child hold the book and turn pages.
    1   2   3

11. I praise my child for spending time reading together.
    1   2   3

12. We take turns reading the book.
    1   2   3

13. I act out the story, use different voices for different characters, or make sound effects.
    1   2   3

14. I keep reading, even after my child loses interest.
    1   2   3

15. I point to pictures, label the pictures, and encourage a response.
    1   2   3

---

ports and present them to the class. Not only does this give parents a chance to share information about books their children enjoyed, but it gives them a chance to practice their own writing.

During the children's literature sessions, one of the things we discuss is how important it is for children and caregivers to experience that books can "talk" to you. When a young child and a parent share a book, they naturally start to talk to each other about what they are reading. Usually the child asks the adult what is happening in the book, and together they figure it out—looking at the pictures, discussing what a new word might mean, remembering what happened on the page before, and guessing what is to come on the next page. Through this, the child learns that reading is not so different from talking.

We also talk about how family reading helps children learn to read themselves, even when they aren't old enough to recognize letters. Without planning it, parents act as models, showing the different things readers do to make sense of a book. When they read with children, adults

- ask questions,
- use pictures to assist in understanding,
- predict what will happen next,
- reread to clarify meaning,
- relate what they read to their own lives,
- act out parts of the story or use different voices for the different characters,
- name and describe objects and events, and
- point out things of special interest.

Parents do these things naturally, without thinking about it. But all of them are examples of what the child can do himself later on, when he starts reading on his own. And because children so often learn by copying, it won't be long before you see your own child doing some of these things when he flips through a book.

Teachers call them "reading strategies." Some of them work best with certain kinds of books. In our program, parents learn about a particular type—or "genre"—of children's literature each week, and we discuss reading strategies that could be helpful with that genre. Parents then try the strategies and genres at home and report back to the class. We hand out home-reading guides each week to help parents observe what goes on with the family reading assignment. While these were developed so that parents in our program could use them when they talked to one another about their experiences, they could be useful to any parent who wants to keep track of family reading. Each guide describes a genre of children's literature and a reading strategy or strategies, and suggests an activity in which the strategies can be used. In addition, the "Recommended Books for Reading With Your Child" list gives some suggestions for books that have been popular in our program, with adults and children alike.

Predictable Books
Briggs, R. (1997). *Jim and the beanstalk*. New York: Putnam.
Carlstrom, N.W. (1986). *Jesse bear, what will you wear?* New York: Macmillan.
Galdone, P. (1981). *The three billy goats gruff*. Boston, MA: Houghton Mifflin.
Keats, E.J. (1971). *Over in the meadow*. New York: Scholastic.
Martin, B. Jr. (1992). *Brown bear, brown bear, what do you see?* New York: Holt, Rinehart.
Robart, R. (1986). *The cake that Mack ate*. Boston, MA: Little, Brown.
Rosen, M. (1990). *We're going on a bear hunt*. New York: Scholastic.

Once Upon a Time Books
Archambault, J., & Martin, B. Jr. (1994). *A beautiful feast for big king cat*. New York: HarperCollins.
Berger, B.H. (1996). *Grandfather Twilight*. New York: Putnam.
Freeman, D. (1968). *A pocket for Corduroy*. New York: Viking.
Hayes, S. (1989). *This is the bear*. Boston, MA: Little, Brown.
McPhail, D. (1972). *The bear's toothache*. Boston, MA: Little, Brown.
Sendak, M. (1988). *Where the wild things are*. New York: HarperCollins.
Wood, D., & Wood, A. (1989). *The little mouse, the red ripe strawberry and the big hungry bear*. Auburn, ME: Child's Play.

Folk Tales and Fables
Galdone, P. (1975). *The ginderbread boy*. New York: Clarion.
Galdone, P. (1979). *The three little pigs*. New York: Clarion.
Galdone, P. (1984). *The elves and the shoemaker*. New York: Clarion.
Galdone, P. (1985). *The three bears*. Boston, MA: Houghton Mifflin.
Mollel, T.M., & Spurll, B. (1992). *Rhinos for lunch and elephants for supper! A Maasai tale*. New York: Clarion.

Wordless Picture Books
Briggs, R. (1978). *The snowman*. New York: Random House.
Day, A. (1985). *Good dog, Carl*. New York: Simon & Schuster.
Felix, M. (1995). *The story of a little mouse trapped in a book*. San Diego, CA: Harcourt Brace.
Hutchins, P. (1968). *Rosie's walk*. New York: Macmillan.
Mayer, M. (1974). *Frog goes to dinner*. New York: Dial.
Turkle, B. (1976). *Deep in the forest*. New York: Dutton.

Concept Books
Hoban, T. (1985). *Is it larger? Is it smaller?* New York: Greenwillow.
Hoberman, M.A. (1985). *A house is a house for me*. New York: Scholastic.
Martin, B. Jr. (1989). *Chicka chicka boom boom*. New York: Simon & Schuster.
McMillan, B. (1988). *Growing colors*. New York: Lothrop.
Rius, M., Parramon, J.M., & Puig, J.J. (1985). *Hearing* (the Five Senses series). New York: Barrons.
Rius, M., Parramon, J.M., & Puig, J.J. (1985). *Touch* (the Five Senses series). New York: Barrons.
Rius, M., Puig, J.J., & Parramon, J.M. (1985). *Sight* (the Five Senses series). New York: Barrons.
Rius, M., Puig, J.J., & Parramon, J.M. (1985). *Smell* (the Five Senses series). New York: Barrons.
Rius, M., Puig, J.J., & Parramon, J.M. (1985). *Taste* (the Five Senses series). New York: Barrons.
Serfozo, M. (1988). *Who said red?* New York: McElderry.

(continued)

Family Stories

Berenstain, S., & Berenstain, J. *The Berenstain Bears series*. New York: Random House.
Bourgeois, P., & Clark, B. *The Franklin series*. New York: Scholastic.
Gilman, P. *The Jillian Jiggs series*. New York: Scholastic.
Maccarone, G. (1992). *Itchy, itchy chicken pox*. New York: Scholastic.
Murphy, J. (1986). *Five minutes' peace*. New York: Putnam.
Slier, D. (1985). *What do toddlers do?* New York: Random House.
Wells, R. (1995). *Edward's overwhelming overnight*. New York: Dial.

Poetry

Brown, M. (1987). *Play rhymes*. New York: Dutton.
dePaola, T. (1985). *Tomie dePaola's Mother Goose*. New York: Putnam.
Katz, M.J. (1990). *Ten potatoes in a pot and other counting rhymes*. New York: HarperCollins.
Lee, D. (1987). *Alligator pie*. Toronto, ON: Gage.
Robinson, F. (Compiler). (1993). *A frog inside my hat: A first book of poems*. New York: Troll.
Sendak, M. (1962). *Chicken soup with rice*. New York: Harper & Row.
Seuss, Dr. (1971). *The lorax*. New York: Random House.

Information Books

Asch, F. (1985). *Bear shadow*. Englewood Cliffs, NJ: Prentice Hall.
Branley, F. (1986). *Air is all around you*. New York: Crowell.
Carle, E. (1984). *The very hungry caterpillar*. New York: Putnam.
Carle, E. (1989). *The very busy spider*. New York: Philomel.
Heller, R. (1981). *Chickens aren't the only ones*. New York: Grosset & Dunlap.
Oppenheim, J., & Reid, B. (1990). *Have you seen birds?* New York: Scholastic.
Simon, N. (1986). *Cats do, dogs don't*. Morton Grove, IL: Albert Whitman.

A reminder: Family reading should be an enjoyable, relaxed time for you and your child. We are not suggesting that you use these strategies in a forced way. It is important that your natural way of reading still be emphasized and that you be flexible in deciding what will work best for you and your child. But by paying attention to particular reading strategies, parents can observe how their children learn and what their children enjoy. This information will let you make reading together in the future an even more positive time.

Predictable Books

This is one of the most common types of children's literature. These stories are simply written, with repeated words, phrases, or sentences, and with a definite pattern or rhythm. They often use familiar sequences (days of the week, numbers) or events that build up one after the other. Examples are old favorites like "The Three Billy Goats Gruff" and "This Is the House That Jack Built" and more recent works such as *Brown Bear, Brown Bear, What Do You See?* by Bill Martin Jr.

Predictable books are very popular with children. Because of the repetition, they quickly become familiar. After only a few readings, children often start to read along, chiming in on the familiar phrases ("I'll huff and I'll puff..."). But even though the writing may be simple, these books still tell a story. Sharing them helps children enter into conversations with books and to realize that reading, listening, and talking aren't so different.

Reading strategy: Dramatizing. Reading with enthusiasm and action makes the experience more fun for your child. Try using a high, squeaky voice for the smallest of the three bears, or blow along with the wolf as he tries to get into the three little pigs' house. It will help hold your child's interest and, if you encourage her efforts to join in, will make her an active participant in the reading. It is one of the simplest and most effective strategies to use, and it works with many genres. With predictable books it is a particularly good thing to try, because repeating actions or voices along with words increases your child's involvement with the book.

Reading strategy: Making predictions. Stop at a key point in the story and ask your child a brief question about what she thinks is going to happen next. You can encourage your child to think carefully by asking something that requires more than a yes or no answer. Starting your question with who, what, where, when, why, or how should do the trick.

Making predictions focuses your child's attention, and it helps her really understand what is happening in the story. Any prediction is the "right" one—make sure to tell your child that, in the world of stories, anything can happen. But if you use this strategy with predictable books, there is a very good chance that she will know *exactly* what is coming, and this will give her early experiences of success in reading.

We read _____

by _____

These are the actions and voices we came up with:

_____

_____

_____

_____

We also guessed what would happen at different parts of the story.

Guess (note who made the guess)   Page

_____

_____

_____

_____

Comments about the book or strategies:

_____

_____

_____

_____

Once Upon a Time...

These books are the familiar, magical ones that children have always loved. You may be able to tell many of the classic stories such as "Cinderella" or "Jack and the Beanstalk" to your child without using a book. The printed versions are written and often illustrated in ways to capture a child's imagination. They tell fantastic stories with colorful pictures and wonderful words, sometimes explaining real-life events (how the leopard got his spots, or what makes thunder) and other times describing something completely made-up (*Where the Wild Things Are* by Maurice Sendak is an example). Reading these stories encourages your child to imagine, pretend, and be creative.

Reading strategy: Asking questions. Stop at an exciting point in the story to ask your child a brief question that requires more than a yes or no answer. What does he think about that funny monster? Why does he think giraffes have those very long necks? When might the tooth-fairy start coming to your house? With "Once Upon a Time" stories, there really never is a single right answer—only a lot of different ones!

Asking questions, like the other strategies, helps keep young children involved and interested in the story, sometimes for much longer than their usual short attention spans. More important, though, it teaches them that they have ideas about the story and it shows them that stories can be related to their own real-life experiences.

We read _____

by _____

These are the questions that were asked:

By you

_____

_____

By me

_____

_____

Comments about the book or strategy:

_____

_____

_____

_____

Folk Tales and Fables

This is another familiar type of children's literature, and the category sometimes overlaps with predictable books and "Once upon a time..." stories. The plots of these books are full of action and involve heroes and villains, a struggle between good and evil, and usually a moral or lesson to be learned. In a fable, this lesson is summed up in one sentence.

Reading strategy: Using picture cues. For young readers, reading is very much about pictures. There are hundreds of beautifully illustrated books of folk tales and fables available, some of which are sure to appeal to your child.

You can help your child understand the story by talking with him about the pictures as you move from page to page. Ask him questions: What do you see in this picture? What is happening? What is that girl doing? How do you think that little bear feels? You'll notice how when you focus on the pictures, lots of questions come into your mind. Your child will soon be able to go beyond simply describing the pictures—he will begin using the pictures to tell the story himself.

We read _____
by _____
We talked about these pictures and what was happening in them:
Page   What's in the picture?

_____

_____

_____

_____

By the end of the book, you were able to help me read these parts:

_____

_____

_____

_____

Comments about the book or strategy:

_____
_____
_____
_____

Wordless Picture Books

When you see a picture in the newspaper or in a magazine, you can often tell a lot about the story behind it without reading the article. Pictures allow us to use our imaginations and become more aware of the feelings behind words.

Children are very "visually oriented"—they learn a great deal about the world by looking and watching. Books without words are perfect for children, especially young toddlers, because they let them concentrate on imagining the story, rather than being sidetracked by printed words. Good wordless picture books, such as those in the "Recommended Books" list, teach children that stories have a beginning, a middle, and an end, and that pictures really can say a thousand words.

Reading strategy: Creating a story using picture cues. As mentioned in the Folk Tales and Fables section, you can use the pictures to create a story. In the case of wordless books, though, the pictures tell the *whole* story. At first, you should try to create the story yourself, using full sentences and asking questions about what you see. Soon your child will join in, suggesting things that might happen next, asking her own questions, and describing characters and events. Encourage her imagination—any story is the right story!

We read _____
by _____
This is the story we created together:

_____
_____
_____
_____

How did your child feel about creating a story?

_____
_____
_____
_____

Comments about the book or strategy:

_____

_____

_____

_____

Concept Books

Concept books are picture books that focus on an idea, such as shape, color, time, the seasons, numbers, or ABCs. They usually show clear, simple pictures of objects related to the concept, with a word or two to label each one. They help children learn the names of many things related to the main idea, to realize that words—spoken and written—are linked to real things, and to break down something into different parts. They are also a great introduction to the skill of putting things into categories. A wide range of these books is available, so you're sure to be able to find one on a topic that really interests your child, whether it's trucks or baby animals.

Reading strategy: Observing and labeling. To help your child learn new words and make links between pictures, words, and "real things," you can ask questions as you share a concept book. If you approach the same concept from a few different angles ("Show me the...," "Is this part of that?," and "Tell me what you see here," for example) you'll also be helping him with problem-solving skills.

We read _____

by _____

What do you see? What else can you tell me?

_____

_____

_____

Comments about the book or strategy:

_____

_____

_____

Family Stories

The best stories are often the ones we hear about our own families. Children love to hear about when their parents were children, and even about themselves when they were babies. What are some stories that you remember about your own parents? What stories might you tell your child about when you were growing up?

Family stories develop the bond of closeness between parent and child and teach about the importance of family. Books about families help children see similarities between storybook events and characters and their own experiences. They also teach about concepts such as growing up, family relationships and routines, and family events such as the birth of a new baby or a move to a new home.

Reading strategy: Relating reading to personal experience. There is perhaps no better way to make reading come alive than to connect book events and personal experience. You can ask questions to help your child make direct links between her everyday experiences and what is happening in the book: "Look at the little boy's toys. Don't you have a ball like that?" "Is this the way you take your bath?" "Oh, oh! Those little bears aren't listening to Mama and Papa. Do you remember when that happened with us in the store?" Helping the child focus on what is similar and different about the story experience and personal experience will increase her comprehension of the book at the same time as it teaches about family concepts.

We read _____

by _____

It reminded us of things in our own family. Here's what we talked about.

What did this book remind you of?

_____
_____
_____
_____

What things happened that are the same in our family?

_____
_____
_____

What things were different?

_____
_____
_____

Comments about the book or strategy:

_____
_____
_____
_____

Poetry

You probably remember many rhymes from your own childhood, and you probably have already told some of them to your child. Young children have fun playing with words that rhyme, so a rhyming story is easy for them to remember. They repeat the rhyme again and again, just to hear the way the words go together. When they do this, they are not just learning the story—they're learning a lot about how the sounds in words are related.

Besides numerous illustrated versions of familiar nursery rhymes like "Mary Had a Little Lamb" or "Jack and Jill Went up the Hill," there are many books of new poetry and rhymes that tell funny, outrageous, or magical stories that children love.

Reading strategy: Rereading. Rereading gives your child many opportunities to hear the rhymes, try to imitate them himself, and really catch the meaning of the poem. Because poems often use odd wording, this can be very important. You will notice yourself that when you reread a poem, you will be a bit more comfortable with it each time and you'll start adding more feeling to the reading. It's the same for children.

At home, you and I read some poems twice. When I asked you what they were about, here's what you told me:

Poem	1st Reading	2nd Reading

Comments about the poems or strategy:

_____

_____

_____

_____

Information Books

Young children are fond of asking "Why?" Quite often their questions are really good ones, and parents can be at a loss to explain. What are some interesting questions your child asks? Have you ever tried to find the answers in a book?

Information books open a whole world of new knowledge to children that can be as exciting and as magical as the world of fairy tales and make-believe. The many good ones available build on what the child already knows and add new ideas in ways that she can really understand. Reading them is not only fun and interesting, but begins to teach the child that books can help her find answers to his questions.

Reading strategy: KL. This is an adaptation of KWL, a strategy used by many elementary school teachers to help older readers organize and remember information they read. The letters stand for what I already *know*, what I *want* to know, and what I *learned*. KL is a simpler strategy parents can use to help young children connect new information with what they already know. This makes the new information easier to understand.

You should show your child how to use this strategy by first demonstrating it. When you pick up a new information book, say something like, "Oh, this one is about caterpillars. I think I already know a bit about this. We've seen caterpillars crawling along the ground, and I know they eat the leaves on our big maple tree. Let's see what else we'll learn about caterpillars from this book." When you try the strategy with your child, ask her directly what she knows about the book's topic. Be sure to accept anything she says. Even if some of her comments don't seem quite right, making them will help her focus on what she can learn from the book. As you read with your child, point out new things about the topic.

We read _____

by _____

Before we started, you told me what you already know about this:

_____

_____

_____

_____

After we read the book, you told me about the new things you learned:

_____

_____

_____

_____

Comments about the book or strategy:

_____

_____

_____

_____

Newspapers

Of course, there are lots of things to read besides books. For example, families often have newspapers in the house—whether it's one that they buy each day or something local that comes free in the mail—and parts of them can make good reading for your child. Best of all, it doesn't matter too much if you cut them up, tear them, or rip out certain pages!

Reading strategy: Parent modeling of reading. Research tells us that when young children see their parents reading for a purpose—to find out when a movie is playing or how to cook the pork chops for dinner, for example—or just for fun, this has positive effect on the children's attitudes toward reading. Children understand that reading is important when the adults at home show that they are really readers. And because they look up to you, they will often want to imitate.

Your child can "read" the newspaper along with you if you make a game out of it. Not only will you be doing something together, but you will be teaching about the different parts of the paper and where things can be found. Try going on a treasure hunt, asking your child to find all the different pictures of food or cars, for example. Cut out pictures and arrange them to make a story. Show your child how to fold the pages neatly. Read the local section and ask your child if he recognizes any of the places or people in the pictures. Many newspapers even contain special sections just for children with stories and related activities. In fact, newspapers today often have education programs. It's not just the weekend comics anymore!

You're never too young to start learning about the world around you. We read these parts of the newspaper together at home:

_____

_____

Here's what happened:

_____

_____

_____

_____

Comments:

_____

_____

_____

_____

Parent-Made Books

In our Family Learning Program, not only do parents explore children's literature and ways to read with their children, they also do their own creative writing, reporting, note taking, and journal writing. This gives the parents a chance to practice their own literacy skills. To make them even more effective, we set up these activities so that they are also related to the children's literacy learning. Besides taking notes about reading strategies and writing reports about children's books, the parents actually make books to share with the children. This gives parents one more way to act as examples to their children, showing them how reading and writing are important and fun for everyone.

Two of the ideas that have been very successful with parents in our program are writing a children's book and making a "memory book."

Writing a Children's Book

Once you have read a variety of children's literature, why not try creating your own story for your child? The published ones can give you ideas of what works and doesn't work with your child. What genre does he like best? What types of pictures does she respond to? Does he like outrageous stories told with rhymes? Does she like action-packed adventures? Thinking about children's likes or fears, their many questions, or an upcoming family event can help parents come up with more ideas.

A concept book can be a good one to try at the start. It's often easy to decide on a concept—your toddler's special interest of the moment (maybe cars or visiting the doctor's office), something she is starting to learn about (the alphabet or the seasons), or something she asks questions about or likes to do with you (helping in the kitchen, plants growing in the garden). Once the concept is set, the writing seems to flow more easily.

Whatever genre you decide to try, remember that writing doesn't happen all at once. It is a process that involves getting and developing the idea, making some notes and drafts, thinking about illustrations, and doing a final copy. The "Tips for Creating Stories" guide suggests a few ways to get organized. These three books could also help:

- Collins, Chase. (1992). *Tell me a story: Creating bedtime tales your children will dream on.* New York: Houghton Mifflin.
- Karl, Jean E. (1994). *How to write and sell children's picture books.* Cincinnati, OH: Writer's Digest Books.
- Stinson, Kathy. (1991). *Writing your best picture book ever.* Markham, ON: Pembroke.

Tips for Creating Stories

1. Draw a line down the center of a page. On the left side, write (in point form) things that happened during the past few days. Write quickly, without thinking. Write whatever comes to mind.

2. Read the left side of the page. If an event brings to mind a story idea—maybe based on an animal, for example—or any extra detail, write it on the right side of the page. Read the left side of the page several times, until you are happy with the story ideas on the right side of the page.

3. Choose a story idea from the right side of the page that would be easy and enjoyable for you to work on and great for your child to hear.

4. Now you are ready to start your first draft. Use short sentences and words that your child will understand (a few challenging words would be fine).

5. If you can, talk to another adult about your idea and the draft. Someone else might be able to think of things that you missed or ways to make the book even better.

6. Decide how your story should appear as a book: Will the words be at the top, middle, or bottom of the page? Which sentences will appear on each page? What sort of illustrations are you going to include?

7. Do as many drafts as you need to until you are satisfied with the story.

8. Rewrite the story on pages that you can put together to make your book. Add the illustrations. Consider going to a copy shop to have the pages laminated.

9. Create a cover for the book, complete with picture, title, and author. Write a dedication and the date on the inside of the cover.

10. Be proud of yourself and enjoy your book with your child!

You also can consider making a book as a coauthor with your child. Work together to come up with the idea. Have him draw the pictures or pick illustrations that can be cut out from magazines or catalogs and glued into your book. So as not to overwhelm your child, don't plan to complete this in one day. He can draw one picture each day or week, depending on his interest and pace. Be ready to step in and help if he wants you to. Then, have your child help tell the story by describing the pictures. You can write down exactly what he says on the page, and he can watch his own words appear "in print."

Memory Books

Most parents cherish their children's early years and agree that they seem to rush by. A family memory book is a way to capture these experiences with young children. A memory book can be a collection of keepsakes like a scrapbook, but in our Family Learning Program it goes beyond that to include writing about early parent-child play, the child's discoveries and learning about language, shared reading, and social development. Each is a unique creation, reflecting a parent's pride in and joy at his or her child's accomplishments. Parents enjoy the project of making these books, and the whole family loves reading the result.

To start a memory book, you can purchase an inexpensive scrapbook at a stationery or department store, or make one with oversize paper and a decorated cardboard cover. Parents in our program have found these suggestions about things to include helpful when they first start thinking about their books:

1. A simple dedication to your child is a special way to start. It could include his name, the span of time covered in the book, and a few words to express your feelings of love, pride, and happiness.

2. Include a biography. Give information about your child's birth, home, family, and "firsts" (first word, first steps, and other major milestones).

3. If you are beginning the book at the child's birth, write about your feelings on the day he was born. If the book begins with another event, write about your special memories of that event and the child's own feelings about it.

4. Children and parents love to look back and remember the things that they enjoyed doing together. You could include sections in which you describe eating, playing, dressing, bed and bath times, and so on.

5. Put in examples of your child's artwork. Write a little about the art activities your child likes best (coloring, painting, playdough, etc.), and talk about how much you see the child learning when he plays.

6. Include a few photographs, and write brief descriptions about where and when they were taken.

7. Write about reading together. Talk about your family reading routines. What is it you like about that time? What are the books that you enjoy together? What are some things you do? How does he react when you're reading with him? How do you react?

Sometimes parents can have "writer's block" when they try to get started on their family memory books. Writing one of the sections as a letter might help you get going. For example, you could write a letter to your daughter about how you felt when you first saw her, or you could write to your son about how proud you were when he first went down the slide on his own at the playground. It is also a good idea to keep ideas for the memory book—mementos, photographs, brief notes to yourself—in a folder. This means that you can have everything close by when planning the layout of your book and revising items. The finished product will give you another book to share with your child, and a keepsake to look at in years to come.

Chapter 5

Parenting

The physical, social, and emotional needs of young children present new challenges for parents every day. When parents get together, they often share ideas and concerns about raising children. "What do you do when...?" are words heard over and over when parents talk to one another.

We believe that parenting should be a priority in family literacy programs, particularly those that involve parents and children regularly over a period of time. When parents have a chance to share their concerns, frustrations, and ideas about being parents, they often learn things that make them better able to cope.

Learning about parenting can also be a good way for parents to put their literacy skills to use. In this chapter we share some of the activities that parents in our program have done. They involve reading, writing, talking and listening, and learning about positive parenting. Specifically, we hope that this chapter will give parents ideas about how to

- offer your child choices, helping her learn to make decisions and develop independence;
- analyze how you relate to your child and what causes conflicts between you;
- figure out positive ways to resolve those conflicts;
- use reading and writing activities as a way to improve your parenting;
- find books and other resources that offer ideas about parenting; and
- develop a home atmosphere based on encouragement, mutual respect, and discipline that is realistic for your child's developmental level.

Foundations for Effective Parenting

There are many books that offer good advice to parents. Some that we recommend are named in the "Parenting Resources" list. Books in this list touch on some of the following topics:

- child development
- health, immunization, nutrition
- safety in the home and on the road, first aid
- toilet training
- sleep habits and bedtime routines
- gender stereotyping
- discipline (setting limits, making rules, using consequences, giving choices, punishing)
- parenting styles
- remembering how you were parented

When we were developing the parenting part of our own family literacy program, we relied particularly on the work of Jean Illsley-Clarke. Her books *Self-Esteem: A Family Affair* and *Growing Up Again* (written with Connie Dawson) talk about family conflicts and how to solve them in ways that protect both parents' and children's self-esteem. These books give examples of four different parenting styles:

- *Structure and nurture*

  In this positive parenting style, the parent gives messages that the child can do things and will be supported. The child learns about how to do things (structure) and that she is cared for (nurture). Parents are clear about "always" ("Don't cross the street without holding my hand") and "usually" ("Bedtime is 8:30") rules. Consequences are fair and established in a context of respect and love (nurture). "If you want to ride your bike, you need to wear a helmet" and "I know you can do it" are examples of things a parent might say in this parenting style.

Parenting Resources

Books

Alexander, S. (Ed.). (1990). *Bringing up our children: Articles from* The Knoxville News. North Billerica, MA: Curriculum Associates.

Crary, E. (1990). *Pick up your socks!* Seattle, WA: Parenting Press.

Crary, E. (1993). *Without spanking or spoiling.* Seattle, WA: Parenting Press.

Essa, E. (1995). *A practical guide to solving preschool behavior problems.* Albany, NY: Delmar.

Faber, A., & Mazlish, E. (1980). *How to talk so kids will listen and listen so kids will talk.* New York: Avon.

Faber, A., & Mazlish, E. (1987). *Siblings without rivalry.* New York: Avon.

Health and Welfare Canada. (1992). *Nobody's perfect* (Leader guide). Ottawa, ON: Ministry of Supply and Services Canada. (See also Wood-Catano, 1992)

Hewitt, D. (1995). *So this is normal too?* St. Paul, MN: Redleaf.

Huntley, R. (1991). *The sleep book for tired parents.* Seattle, WA: Parenting Press.

Illsley-Clarke, J. (1978). *Self-esteem: A family affair.* San Francisco, CA: HarperCollins.

Ilsley-Clarke, J. (1981). *Self-esteem: A family affair* (Leader guide). San Francisco, CA: HarperCollins.

Illsley-Clarke, J., & Dawson, C. (1989). *Growing up again: Parenting ourselves, parenting our children.* Center City, MN: Hazelden Educational Materials.

Illsley-Clarke, J., Kemp, S., Nordeman, G., & Petersen, E. (1986). *Help! For parents of infants from birth to 6 months.* New York: Harper & Row.

Manolson, A. (1995). *You make the difference.* Toronto, ON: Hanen Centre.

Wood-Catano, J. (1992). *Nobody's perfect* (Booklet series). Ottawa, ON: Health and Welfare Canada, Ministry of Supply and Services. (See also Health and Welfare Canada, 1992)

Videotapes

Colorosso, B. (1989). *Winning at parenting...without beating your kids.* Littleton, CO: Kids Are Worth It.

Common childhood illnesses. (1991). Charleston, WV: Cambridge Research Group.

Dinkmeyer, D., & McKay, G. (1989). *Early childhood STEP (Systematic Training for Effective Parenting of Children Under Six).* Circle Pines, MN: American Guidance Services.

The ouchless house: Baby safe your home. (1992). Charleston, WV: Cambridge Research Group.

Phelan, T.W. (1990). *1, 2, 3, magic.* Glen Ellyn, IL: Child Management.

Shaking, hitting, spanking: What to do instead. (1990). Lake Zurich, IL: Learning Seed.

- *Criticism*

  This style scolds the child rather than providing standards for acceptable behavior. Criticism often includes all-encompassing words such as "never" and "always." At its worst, this style ridicules, mocks, and derides. An example of this style is saying something like "If you wet your pants again, I'll put you back in diapers, because you're just like a baby."

- *Marshmallow parenting*

  Here, the parent gives the child a lot of freedom but doesn't expect responsibility. It sounds supportive, but it implies that the child does not have to or is incapable of following rules. It discounts the child's ability and gives permission for irresponsibility and failure. At the same time, it lets the parent look good, play the martyr, or feel in control. A marshmallow parent might say, "She can eat whatever she wants. I always had to eat what was put out. You're only a child once."

- *Abandonment*

  This is a style of no rules, protection, or contact. It tells the child that you are not available. Teasing is often part of this style. Here a parent might say, "I'm fed up. You can go to bed whenever you're tired."

All parents experience frustration or anger sometimes, and all of us recognize these parenting styles as things we've used ourselves. In addition, we all have our own beliefs and attitudes about how to raise children. We developed the "About Parents and Kids" survey to help parents in our program think about their own ideas and styles of parenting. There are no right or wrong answers, but the responses you choose may indicate a preference for one of the four parenting styles.

We hope that by focusing on ways of parenting and by doing the following activities, parents may begin to rely more often on structure and nurture than on the other styles.

Group Discussion

Parents often say that one of the best ways to learn about parenting is to share ideas with other caregivers and parents. As one parent in our program noted, "When everyone is in the same boat, you don't feel so alone."

About Parents and Kids

Below are statements that some parents think are true. Other parents disagree.
Read each one and decide if it is true for you. Remember: There are no right or wrong answers.

Circle the number that best describes how you feel about each sentence. 1 means you strongly agree, 2 means you agree, 3 means "maybe," 4 means you disagree, and 5 means you disagree strongly.

1. Single parents don't have time to play with their children.
    1   2   3   4   5

2. Children should be seen and not heard.
    1   2   3   4   5

3. Parents can't really control children these days. There is too much outside influence.
    1   2   3   4   5

4. Parents have to set limits for children, but it should be done without ever yelling.
    1   2   3   4   5

5. Children are never too young to share responsibilities and duties around the house.
    1   2   3   4   5

6. A spank now and then gives the child the right message about who is boss.
    1   2   3   4   5

7. Parents should be in charge of setting the routines for children when it comes to eating, sleeping, dress, etc.
    1   2   3   4   5

8. Give kids freedom when they are young—life will be hard enough when they get older.
    1   2   3   4   5

9. Parents should make sure boys act like boys, otherwise they could become sissies or worse.
    1   2   3   4   5

10. Be very strict with children—if you give them an inch, they will take a yard.
    1   2   3   4   5

11. These days parents feel they are at their wits' end most of the time.
    1   2   3   4   5

12. A mother always has a special relationship with her daughter, because a daughter will have the feelings of a woman.
    1   2   3   4   5

13. Let a child know he's bad when he has done something. At least he might be ashamed.
    1   2   3   4   5

14. Girls should act like girls—more quiet, play with girl things, and help around the house.
    1   2   3   4   5

(continued)

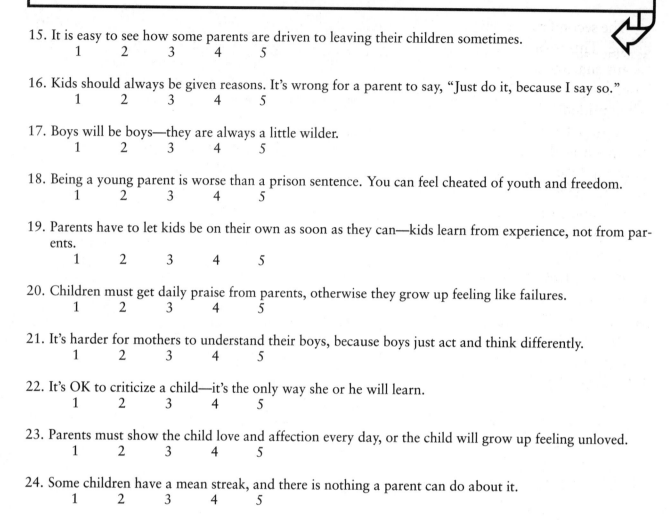

15. It is easy to see how some parents are driven to leaving their children sometimes.
    1   2   3   4   5

16. Kids should always be given reasons. It's wrong for a parent to say, "Just do it, because I say so."
    1   2   3   4   5

17. Boys will be boys—they are always a little wilder.
    1   2   3   4   5

18. Being a young parent is worse than a prison sentence. You can feel cheated of youth and freedom.
    1   2   3   4   5

19. Parents have to let kids be on their own as soon as they can—kids learn from experience, not from parents.
    1   2   3   4   5

20. Children must get daily praise from parents, otherwise they grow up feeling like failures.
    1   2   3   4   5

21. It's harder for mothers to understand their boys, because boys just act and think differently.
    1   2   3   4   5

22. It's OK to criticize a child—it's the only way she or he will learn.
    1   2   3   4   5

23. Parents must show the child love and affection every day, or the child will grow up feeling unloved.
    1   2   3   4   5

24. Some children have a mean streak, and there is nothing a parent can do about it.
    1   2   3   4   5

Key:
These statements relate to the criticizing style of parenting: 2, 6, 10, 13, 22, 24
These statements relate to setting limits and providing structure: 4, 5, 7, 16
These statements relate to nurturing: 20, 23
These statements relate to the marshmallow style of parenting: 3, 8, 19
These statements talk about stress: 1, 11, 15, 18
These statements talk about gender stereotyping: 9, 12, 14, 17, 21

When any group gets together, there are ways to make sure the conversation is positive, supportive, and constructive. Besides talking about problems or concerns, we try to remember to take time during our group discussions to talk about positive things, too—whether to recall feelings of love at the birth of a baby, or pride at that baby's development into a young child. It's also useful to keep in mind two basic rules:

1. Speak positively about one another.
2. Keep confidences confidential, and don't gossip.

The second rule is particularly important for discussions about parenting. This is obviously a very personal subject, and talking about it means sharing confidences. Parents who participate in group discussions must recognize their responsibility to be supportive and honor the confidential nature of whatever is shared. If the discussion takes place in a formal setting—like an organized program or support group—it is also important for the parents to know that the teachers or group leaders will make sure that privacy is respected. On the other hand, parents should never feel that they have to discuss things they would rather keep to themselves. A successful group discussion can happen only in an atmosphere where everyone feels comfortable about participating.

In our program, we have a "suggestion circle," a technique for organizing group discussions developed by Jean Illsley-Clarke. One group member volunteers to share a problem or concern he or she has about parenting, and other group members take turns suggesting ideas and possible solutions. Here are some of the things parents have raised in our group:

> "I can't get Amy to go to bed on time. She dawdles and I get mad."
> "Jeff won't stay in his own room at night. He always ends up in our bed."
> "I can't stand Trevor's whining instead of asking."
> "Gina is a picky eater. She never eats what I give her."
> "Beth should be toilet trained by now. She's three and I think she's just lazy about it."
> "Lindsey is mean to her younger sister. She's always pinching and teasing."

Often, other parents have experience of the same issue and can tell what they did to address it in their own families. One of us writes down the ideas, and the volunteer agrees to think about them and try one or more out at home.

The suggestion circle format includes a few things to keep in mind when discussing a problem. These could apply to any group discussion, whether it's part of a suggestion circle or something more casual:

- show respect for others
- let other people have a chance to talk
- respect confidentiality
- focus on "here-and-now" problems
- offer constructive ideas to help
- be positive and try to compliment others whenever possible

Keeping a Journal

Of course, it's not always possible to share problems and concerns with other parents, and often you may not want to. Keeping a personal journal of reflections and observations about your family, parenting concerns, questions, and plans gives you a chance to think about your day-to-day experiences with your child. Although in our Family Learning Program many parents choose to share their journals with the teacher, doing so is not required. In fact, journal writing is an excellent way to express private thoughts that you want to keep private. Journal writing lets you review what you are learning about your child and about yourself, and it gives you time to think about family concerns and to develop possible solutions. And, of course, it lets you practice your own writing and express your creativity.

We suggest to parents that they organize their journal writing around four topics—Myself, Learning, Home Time, and Parenting—and write about each of them each week. In order to make getting underway a little easier, we have developed the following sentence starters, organized around these topics:

- *Myself*

    I would like to make some changes....
    I'm tired of....
    I think I'm going to....
    I wonder how I would go about getting....
    Something happened that made me feel good....
    I really like it when I....
    One of the things I've learned from experience is....
    It bugs me when....
    I don't know what to do about....

- *Learning*

    My daughter likes to count everything now....
    My son washed his own hands today....
    Today when we were reading, he recognized his own name in the book....
    Yesterday I saw her share a toy in the playground....
    I'm a little worried because the other kids in her playgroup talk better than she does....

- *Home time*

    We've been watching so much television that I've decided to....
    When we are getting ready for bed, my daughter goes right for a book....
    We had a great conversation the other day....

He's really trying to help a lot around the house now....

• *Parenting*

My son is biting....

My daughter is starting to wet the bed at night. Last night she....

I tried a time out with him yesterday, but it didn't work very well....

This morning we were making his bed, and out of the blue he said, "I got a pretty Mom." I felt....

Yesterday I was kind of down. She must have been able to tell because she said, "Why you sad?" We talked about....

Once you get started and are really in the routine of keeping a journal, you'll usually find that the writing flows out. Parents are keen observers of their children, and being a parent gives you plenty of things to write about.

Problem Solving

You and your child are learning about each other all the time. Sometimes things go smoothly and both of you enjoy being together. At other times it can be rough going. Parents need to have good problem-solving skills for those challenging times. They need to be able to figure out positive ways of handling conflicts, with effective solutions that keep harmony in the family.

Elizabeth Crary, one of the authors listed in the "Parenting Resources" chart, has a simple five-step guide to help parents solve problems with their toddlers and preschoolers:

• Step 1: Identify a concern, observe, and clarify.
• Step 2: Use an "ABC" analysis—what happens *after*, what happened *before*, what are the *consequences*.
• Step 3: Consider the options.
• Step 4: Develop an action plan.
• Step 5: Keep track of progress.

Crary's books also help parents think about different solutions and give examples of parenting techniques such as reinforcement, time out, modeling, ignoring, and redirecting. Some of these techniques are summarized in the "Parenting Strategy Checklist" on the next page.

We adapted Crary's problem-solving approach as the basis of a parent problem-solving project. Parents in our program select areas they

Parenting Strategy Checklist

Never Give Up!

Get out of a rut and try something new. Think about creative ways to do the following:

1. Avoid problems before they happen
   - reduce boredom
   - change time, place, activity
   - plan transitions (bath, bedtime, meals, leaving home)
   - prepare him or her for the new or the unpleasant
   - express clear expectations by understanding the child's present level, speaking at that level, and changing questions to commands
   - offer limited choice rather than free choice
   - use guided choice
   - use Grandma's Rule: Follow a difficult behavior with a pleasant consequence ("If you eat your spinach, you can have some ice cream.")

2. Change what's being rewarded
   - "catch 'em" being good
   - substitute a positive for a negative consequence
   - use a time out as an alternative
   - praise more frequently

3. Find a way to teach new behavior
   - modeling
   - shaping
   - redoing it right
   - practicing
   - looking for "a better way" together

4. Change misbehavior*
   - ignoring
   - offering a substitution

*Be sure you understand the possible goals of misbehavior. Is the child looking for attention? If so, these strategies might be appropriate.

---

wish to change, and they write about their experiences using the 5-step guide. Over the 4 or 5 weeks that we work on this, parents become familiar with some approaches and strategies that may help with those rough times at home. They try out new ideas for problem solving and share what they learn with other parents. Along the way, they make notes of what they see happening with their children, and use these notes to keep track of how their new approaches are working.

In our program, talking about ideas and experiences with other parents is an important part of the project. We hope, however, that all parents—even those who don't have the opportunity to meet regularly with other parents—will be able to use this approach to finding new ways to solve problems with their children. Many parents say things like, "This is not a big problem. I can handle it." Nevertheless, it can help to have some ideas and suggestions to let you get beyond simply "handling" it. A different way can be easy to try and result in a positive change for you. You will be surprised at how much better you feel when you start *solving* problems and not just coping with them.

The remainder of this chapter is a step-by-step guide to this approach. Overall, the steps are as follows:

1. Identify a specific concern and observe the circumstances that relate to it (the what, when, where, and how of the problem).

2. Describe the ABCs of the problem.

3. Think of as many solutions as possible. Try to get ideas from other parents if you can, and use books, videos, magazine articles, and so on. Decide on a strategy that you think can improve your particular problem.

4. Make a plan for trying the new strategy.

5. Try out your plan for a week. Keep a record of what you do and how your child responds. After the week is up, do a "tune up" and make some changes if you need to.

The following worksheets can help you keep notes, collect ideas, record your observations, and summarize your conclusions.

Step 1: Identify and Observe

As children grow and change, we have to change our ways of parenting. Before we can do this, we need to see and tell about what is really happening with our children and to clearly identify our particular concerns.

Here are some common parenting concerns. Is there something that sounds like your concern?

- My child lies a lot.
- My child is a picky eater.
- My child always wants his own way.
- My child never picks up her toys.
- My child hits other children.
- My child is very nervous.
- My child is very dependent.

What is a parenting concern you have? If you can, pair up with another parent, and interview each other about something that bugs you about managing your child. Whether you are working on your own or with a partner, make sure that the problem you are thinking about is something that has been going on for a while. Be open. Don't be embarrassed. Every parent has difficult moments and hard-to-handle situations.

Jot down some notes to answer the following questions. At this point, don't worry about spelling, grammar, or using sentences—these are words just to help you focus your thinking and for remembering later.

What is the problem?

_____

_____

_____

What does your child do?

_____

_____

_____

When does it happen during the day? Where does it go on?

_____

_____

_____

How long has it been going on? How often does it happen?

_____

_____

_____

What do you do when it happens?

_____

_____

_____

How do you feel about it?

_____

_____

_____

Now try to sum up your parenting concern. (Again, this is for you, so don't worry about spelling or grammar.) Use the notes you made, and give some details about what your child does that you want to change. Try to use action words such as *yells*, *hits*, or *wets the bed*. Stay away

from value words like *moody, mean,* or *clingy* that don't describe what
your child does.

_____

_____

_____

Step 2: Using the ABCs

Now that you have identified your parenting concern and said how
your child acts, take a closer look at events before and after the problem behavior. This will help you learn about all the things that trigger
the behavior you want to change. You also want to know why your
son or daughter behaves this way. What are the consequences? What
does she want to get? Is he looking for attention, praise, something
new to do, a special treat? What is she trying to avoid? Is he worried
about being scolded or punished?

When you know the ABCs—what went on before, what happens
after, and what are the consequences—you can make a good choice
about what to do.

Review the notes you made in step 1, just to be clear about what
it is that your child does. Working with a partner or on your own,
think about what is going on when the behavior occurs. Jot down
notes about the following questions.

What is the behavior you want to work on?

_____

_____

_____

What happens just before the behavior? What do you think your child
is looking for?

_____

_____

_____

What are you doing when the behavior happens?

_____

_____

_____

What happens immediately after your child behaves this way? What
are the immediate results?

_____

_____

_____

What do you do right after it happens?

_____
_____
_____

What rewards or punishments do you give?

_____
_____
_____

Step 3: Consider the Options

Of course, you want to choose the best strategy to help you solve the problem, but deciding on one can be confusing. Before you choose, look at all the options.

At this stage, you need to sit down and make a list of all the possible things you could do. Talk to other parents to get ideas, consult books and other resources, reread the "Parenting Strategy Checklist," and use your own experience. Write down *everything*. Keep an open mind, and don't strike anything off your list thinking, "That won't work."

Here are six things I could try. (Write even more possibilities on another sheet of paper if you can.)

_____
_____
_____
_____
_____
_____

After you have brainstormed all the possible solutions, go back and think about each one. How do you think each one might work in your situation? Talk with another parent if you can. Sometimes an outside opinion can help.

Now, try to decide on a number 1 and 2 choice to try with your child.
1._____
2._____

Step 4: My Action Plan

You have described the problem, thought about the possible solutions, and decided on something to try. Now you are ready to develop an action plan.

The action plan is a way of focusing directly on the problem and what you're going to do about it. Write responses to the following in order to create a summary.

I would like to change this behavior of my child:

_____

_____

_____

Here is a summary of the ABCs of this behavior:

_____

_____

_____

My conclusion from these observations is that my child behaves this way because

_____

_____

_____

_____

Here is the strategy I'm going to use to try to change this behavior:

_____

_____

_____

_____

This is how I will put the strategy into effect:

_____

_____

_____

_____

I think this is the best strategy because

_____

_____

_____

_____

Step 5: Keeping Track

Use your plan for 2 weeks. The first week is a try-out. In the second week, you can fine-tune your approach if you need to, or you can try out the strategy that was your second choice (see step 3) if things really aren't getting better.

Use the following outline to record what happens.

Week 1

Date: _____

What happened to my plan? How did my plan work?

_____

_____

_____

Did the behavior get better? Stay the same? Get worse?

_____

_____

_____

What did my child do?

_____

_____

_____

What did I do?

_____

_____

_____

Were there any specific problems with the plan?

_____

_____

_____

Do I need to make changes? What changes might help?

_____

_____

_____

Week 2

Date: _____

What happened to my plan this week? How did my plan work?

_____

_____

_____

Did the behavior get better? Stay the same? Get worse?

_____

_____

_____

What did my child do?

_____

_____

_____

What did I do?

_____

_____

_____

Overall, has this strategy helped?

_____

_____

_____

What could I try next? Is there another problem that I could try to solve? Another strategy to use for this problem or a different one?

_____

_____

_____

A Final Word

Our children are very precious. We want to help and guide them to independence and a life filled with personal satisfaction and empathy for others. Today, more than ever, the profound influence of the family on children's learning is being recognized. Although families may come in all sizes—extended or nuclear, headed by a single parent or blended—nothing can replace the teaching relationship between primary caregivers and children. All children are born with enormous potential to think, create, express ideas, and solve problems. This potential is developed first at home through shared experiences with family.

As parents, we know it is the little things that count. The memory of a few minutes spent talking with our children about how they see the world around them can be cherished years later. These moments, taken together, become thousands of hours in which children are learning. We hope this book has been helpful to you, the parents and caregivers who want to nurture your children's learning by including more reading and writing in your family lives.